THE ENTERPRISING SCOT

THE ENTERPRISING SCOT

SCOTTISH ADVENTURE AND ACHIEVEMENT

EDITED BY JENNI CALDER

ROYAL MUSEUM OF SCOTLAND

EDINBURGH
HER MAJESTY'S STATIONERY OFFICE

309760

Frontispiece

Banknote from the
collections of the
National Museums of
Scotland. The Royal
Bank of Scotland was
founded in 1727. The
Scots were pioneers in
banking, and Scottish
banks played a leading
role in industrial and
commercial
development. (NMS)

ISBN 0 11 492483 X

CONTENTS

PREFACE

In October 1985 the National Museums of Scotland were brought into being as a result of the union between the former National Museum of Antiquities of Scotland and the Royal Scottish Museum and their smaller satellite museums. Both the National Museum of Antiquities of Scotland and the Royal Scottish Museum have distinguished histories. The first began in 1780 as the museum of the Society of Antiquaries, the second in 1854 as the Industrial Museum of Scotland, becoming successively the Edinburgh Museum of Science and Art and the Royal Scottish Museum. All these institutions, whose names appear in the text, are now part of the National Museums of Scotland.

To commemorate and to demonstrate this important merger, it was decided to present a major special exhibition in the summer of 1986. The theme was 'The Enterprising Scot', a view of Scottish achievement expressed through the collections of Scotland's National Museums. It was shown at the Royal Scottish Academy in Edinburgh, once the home of the National Museum of Antiquities of Scotland, during August and September 1986.

The Enterprising Scot, published in conjunction with the exhibition, reflects the diversity of the collections and the comprehensive interests of the National Museums of Scotland.

ACKNOWLEDGEMENTS

A book of this kind is the result of collective and cooperative effort. Many individuals have contributed in diverse ways to the gathering of information and material that appears in these pages. I would like to record my grateful appreciation to all the contributors whose names appear, to the Museums' photographers Ian Larner and Ken Smith, and to Godfrey Evans, Janis Kemp, Ian Lyster, Allen Simpson, Naomi Tarrant and Jane Wilkinson, also of the staff of the National Museums of Scotland. I am grateful to Therese Duriez for carrying out the picture research under difficult circumstances; thanks also to George Deas Brown of Hobart, Tasmania and Sara Stevenson and Julie Lawson of the Scottish National Portrait Gallery, Edinburgh.

I would like to add my personal thanks to Sheila Brock, Pat Macdonald and Geoff Swinney for their support and advice.

JC

INTRODUCTION

Jenni Calder

Scotland has always been a frontier country. Poised between Continental Europe and Scandinavia, there have been strong associations with both. It has been regarded by England as a northern outpost, often troublesome, always different from the style and habits of southern Britain. Perhaps because of its frontier nature, subject to contrasting influences and torn by conflicting impulses, Scotland has supplied the world with pioneering individuals and ideas which have made a distinctive contribution. Many have commented that this contribution has been beyond all reasonable expectations of a small and often struggling country.

The exploration of why Scotland, so limited in resources and often regarded as more pugnacious than productive, should occupy so bold a position on the map of world achievement will continue. This book does not set out to be a comprehensive charting of the territory of the enterprising Scot, but looks at some aspects of Scottish achievement. A number of these have been much celebrated, others may be entirely new to the reader. We hope that by bringing together a diversity of people, places and activities we are inviting a fresh look at Scotland's contribution to the world. The fact that there is much more to be said is a further tribute to Scottish enterprise.

Before the end of the eighteenth century, which saw at last the political partnership of Scotland and England, Scots had a reputation of being hard fighters and independent thinkers. Those who went abroad, and many did, were highly regarded for their individualism as well as business-like astuteness. The tradition of the enduring and independent Scot survived through the growth and consequences of industrialisation. Many were pioneers of progress in their own land, both inventive and adventurous in their application of new ideas, whatever their source. The story of the dramatic growth of commerce and production, first after the Union of the Parliaments in 1707, then with the spread of industrialism, is the story of the enterprise not only of manufacturers, merchants and financiers, but the application and adaptability of thousands of men and women.

But enterprise is not the sole preserve of the movers of capital, nor of those who fuel that movement. Scotland's impact on the world has been made as much through ideas, creativity and religious conviction as through the products of industry and business acumen. In the first half of the nineteenth century the kingdom of cotton in Scotland was followed by the sovereignty of iron and steel, but the best known Scottish names in Europe and North America at that time were probably those of Robert Burns, poet, and Walter Scott, novelist.

It has often been suggested that the Scottish terrain and the Scottish climate between them bred a particular hardiness. Much of Scotland, however beautiful, is bleak and unproductive. The drover who herded black cattle, one of the few sellable commodities of the Highlands before the arrival of sheep, sportsmen and tourists, over hundreds of miles to a lucrative English market could subsist on a handful of oatmeal mixed with water from the burn. Terrain and climate may also have helped to breed a hardiness of conviction. Clan and family loyalties and religious faith both bound Scots together and divided them with a ferocity that lingered long after the disintegration of the clan system and religious contention had become less aggressively expressed if no less deeply felt.

These contradictory pressures were significant impulses, direct and indirect, in many aspects of Scottish achievement. Such contradictions also made Scotland vulnerable, and lent themselves to exploitation as well as to enterprise. 'I should imagine,' wrote General Wolfe in 1751, 'that two or three independent Highland companies might be of use; they are hardy, intrepid, accustomed to a rough country, and no great mischief if they fall.' Thus the military establishment was ready to take advantage of the defeat of the Jacobites in 1746 to help Britain to victory over the French in 1759.

While the Scottish soldier, and often the Scottish settler, became expendable tools in the construction of an empire, Scottish courage and alacrity brought striking commercial success abroad. The Scottish contribution to British expansion and influence in North America, in Africa, in India and the Far East, in Australia and the Pacific, was so great as to suggest that the Scots were as often the architects as the tools of empire building. They not only fought, bought and sold, but were the purveyors of a vast range of knowledge and experience. The skills of Scottish missionaries and doctors, engineers and explorers, teachers and administrators, linguists and legislators, have imprinted minds as well as maps throughout the world.

The raw materials of Scottish achievement lay, both literally and metaphorically, in the land itself. The harsh contours of the Highlands were the source not only of crofters and soldiers, but of fishermen, seamen, explorers, adventurers, and many thousands of settlers in foreign lands. The Clyde, the Forth and the Tay rivers were the focus of industrial activity, and from them sailed the ships that took the results of that industry all over the world, and returned with the commodities that helped to build great fortunes and great cities. The gentler, fertile fields of lowland Scotland have been the scene not only of the rigorous application of the farmer, but also of experiment and innovation. The face of Scotland is as scarred as any other area of the developed world by the hand of man, but the country's essential character remains. That character has helped to shape the Scottish people, who in turn have helped to shape countries as disparate as New Zealand and India.

In 1872 the son of a tenant farmer near Kelso set out for North America, frustrated by 'the neglect of ability, the silent, sarcastic repression of any forward movement, the absence of a generous uplift' which he felt characterised the country he was leaving. His name was John Clay, and by the end of the century he was an extremely successful cattle rancher in Wyoming. Many would have agreed with his view of Victorian Scotland as repressive, reluctant to foster productive talents and abilities, and many left on that account. Yet much of Scottish success, even that which was the result of the scope provided by new territories, owed a great deal to factors that have been identified as particularly Scottish. One was the belief, endorsed by Calvinism, that hard work was both materially and spiritually rewarding. The other was a broadly-based education

Rothiemurchus. The rugged landscapes of the Highlands enforced a rugged life, which helped to shape the Scottish character. (NMS)

Lothian farmland. For centuries the Lothians have been an important area of grain and vegetable production, which has helped to feed populous central Scotland. (Pat Macdonald)

The Forth Valley, looking across Grangemouth to the west. The Firth of Forth saw Scotland's earliest development of industrial and shipping activity. (Pat Macdonald)

system which in theory, if not always in practice, gave opportunities and encouragement beyond that which was customary in the rest of Europe.

John Clay, like Andrew Carnegie who might well have lived out his life as a Dunfermline weaver, believed he could succeed, and even if neither felt that success would come in Scotland it is likely that both owed that belief to their Scottish origins. Without such conviction enterprise, on however modest a scale, can hardly begin.

Today neither the character nor the extent of Scottish enterprise is questioned, although there is much yet to be discovered about how and why it operated. There are many neglected areas; to some of these we have drawn attention here. We have looked at some of the more unassuming contributions as well as the well known, at aspects of collective enterprise as well as notable individuals. Our time span rests mainly within the eighteenth and nineteenth centuries, but that should not be seen to suggest either a beginning or an end to Scottish enterprise. Our interests reflect also the concerns of the National Museums of Scotland, themselves monuments to the enterprising Scot. Without the energy and adventurousness and the spirit of enquiry of Scots at home and abroad these museums would never have developed into the important and distinctive institutions they now are. If many of those who contributed to their country's world of learning did so through circumstances forced by necessity rather than by choice, our respect for their marked ability to respond creatively under duress can only be heightened. Enterprise, as we have seen, is not just the province of the privileged, nor is it always the result of design.

In 1775 the Englishman Edward Topham was visiting Edinburgh. 'Go into whatever country you will,' he wrote from that city in a letter to a friend, 'you will always find Scotchmen.' And he went on:

> They penetrate into every climate: you meet them in all the various departments of travellers, soldiers, merchants, adventurers, domestics. Consult the history of their own nation from the earliest period, and that of other nations, and you will find that if any dangerous and difficult enterprise has been undertaken, any uncommon proofs given of patience or activity, any new countries visited and improved, that a Scotchman has borne some share in the performance.

Much of Scotland's enterprise has brought little reward to Scotland. But Scotland's loss is the world's gain. If at times there has not been enough space or elasticity in Scotland to accommodate all the talents, ideas and willingness of the Scottish people we should remember that Scotland itself has been a challenge to generations of enterprising Scots. The story of Scottish achievement is the story of those who rose to that challenge, as well as of those who sought new frontiers.

What follows is an anthology of pieces on the theme of Scottish adventure and achievement, both in Scotland and in some of the distant parts of the world where Scots have had an impact. Six major articles highlight a number of key aspects of Scottish impact, while shorter pieces look at individuals and areas of enterprise ranging from engineers to artists, from commerce to collecting. Between each piece there is an illustrated link that extends the story of Scottish enterprise.

*The wandering Scot took his culture with him. Gilbert Kerr,
naturalist and taxidermist aboard the* Scotia, *which sailed on
the Scottish National Antarctic Expedition in 1902 under
William Bruce, plays to a captive audience. The scene, Coats
Land, was named after the Coats family, thread makers of
Paisley, who helped to fund the expedition.*

SCOTLAND: THE WORLD PERSPECTIVE

George Shepperson

In the period of Scottish history which begins with the Union of the Parliaments of Scotland and England in 1707, by which the Scots achieved 'full Freedom and Intercourse of Trade and Navigation to and from . . . the Dominions and Plantations' of the expanding English overseas empire, Scots made a mark on the world which has yet to be put into its proper perspective. It is to the many episodes and incidents of two and a half centuries of the Anglo-Scottish Union that those writers who concern themselves with Scottish influences upon the world usually turn their attention. But the effect of this post-1707 approach has been that many students of Scottish history tend to overlook the influence of Scots abroad in the period before the Union. The readiness of Scots to migrate to Europe, permanently or temporarily, in the medieval and Reformation periods before 1707, in search of economic and social advancement, learning or just sheer adventure, built up a momentum of migration which enabled them to take full advantage of all the opportunities which legal entry into the British Empire after 1707 bestowed upon them.

Yet the pre-1707 period of Scottish emigration and enterprise abroad did not have an exclusively European orientation. As the countries of Europe in the fifteenth, sixteenth and seventeenth centuries sought to take advantage of the opportunities for national and individual advancement which the discoveries of courageous seamen

Robert Louis Stevenson with his family and workers at Vailima, Samoa. Stevenson's years of exile were highly productive. (By Courtesy of Edinburgh Central Library)

such as Christopher Columbus and Vasco da Gama had opened up, Scottish sailors, soldiers, settlers, traders and adventurers followed similar paths. Throughout the seventeenth century in particular, Scottish settlers and adventurers were attracted to the Americas, from Nova Scotia in the north to New Caledonia on the Isthmus of Darien, near Panama. It seemed that a separate Scottish overseas empire was in the making; but the dice were loaded against Scotland, especially by the more successful maritime gamblers of England. Scotland had to become a partner in the English overseas empire — whether a junior partner or the exponent of one of the most successful takeover bids in history is still a matter for emotive opinion — before Scottish enterprise could flourish in the Americas, Africa, Asia and Australasia.

Scots did, however, indulge in one successful colonial venture before the Union — although, like all so-called 'successful' colonial schemes, it was one which has brought upon both colonists and colonised their share of suffering. This was the settlement of Scots in the north of Ireland. Beginning in the first decade of the seventeenth century, it had reached the near million mark by the last decade. Although sovereignty lay in the crown of England, Ulster, as Professor Dewar Gibb declared in his *Scottish Empire*, 'is Scotland's most successful colony'. A hardy, self-reliant, strongly Protestant breed, the Scots in the north of Ireland displayed both the virtues and the vices of Scottish settlement abroad. Of the latter characteristics, Professor Dewar Gibb speaks bluntly: 'What was the attitude of these Scottish settlers towards the "natives"?' There is no doubt about the answer. It embraces the perennial judgement of the Scot upon the Irishman. Their attitude was one of contempt for those who throughout the official correspondence of the time are referred to as 'the mere Irish'. And it seems that that attitude was encouraged from above. The colonists kept together and did not intermarry with the Irish. 'They were of a superior race and they meant to keep that race pure.' When many of the Ulster Scots went over to the British American colonies in the eighteenth century, they took a similar culture pattern with them. These Scotch-Irish, as they used to be called, having won their spurs as settlers on the frontier in Ireland, went on to make a distinctive contribution to the frontier in America and to Presbyterianism and political liberty in the independent American tradition. But these hardy pioneers were also inclined to take justice into their own hands. To them is attributed the introduction of Lynch law into America in 1763

The massive migration out of Scotland, in the two and a half centuries after the union, of individuals, institutions and ideas — and they sometimes travelled together and sometimes independently — is one of the wonders of modern times. There are formidable difficulties in the way of arriving at an accurate estimate, not the least of which is the unreliability of British migration statistics before the middle of the nineteenth century. But we know for certain that thousands left Scotland, and through this many-faceted migration Scotland has made an ineradicable mark on the development of the modern world. The wandering of Scots away from home has often been compared to the dispersal of the Jews; and out of this has come what Sir Reginald Coupland called 'the Scottish Diaspora'. One of the most percipient observers of the Scot abroad, as well as an outstanding example of the peripatetic Scot in many countries, Robert Louis Stevenson, made his own characteristic comment on the Scottish Diaspora: 'It is at least a curious thing . . . that the races which wander the widest, Jews and Scotch, should be the most clannish in the world. But perhaps these two are cause and effect: "for ye were strangers in the land of Egypt".'

The use of Biblical language serves to remind us of one of the greatest, perhaps the greatest, contributions by Scots to world history: their role in the dissemination of religious and religious-derived ideas and institutions overseas. Much of this, of course, comes from the thorough-going nature of the Reformation in Scotland, with its emphasis on the spread of education in order that even the humblest folk might read the Scriptures; its establishment of the Presbyterian form of Church government; and its stimulus to theological debate amongst people of all classes and callings.

The transport overseas of the essential elements of the Reformation in Scotland began before 1707. But it was greatly accelerated after the Union by the intensification of emigration from Scotland. This placed a Presbyterian mark on many areas of the expanding English-speaking world, especially in those countries which became the United States of America and Canada, influencing the emergence of democracy in State as well as in Church. Much, but by no means all, of this Presbyterianism was disseminated overseas from Scotland in the eighteenth century and in the first half of the nineteenth. Variations on the Presbyterian theme abroad were provided after the Disruption in the established Church of Scotland in 1843, through which the Free Church came into existence, particularly after the arrival of solidly Scottish settlers at Otago in 1848, intent on turning this part of New Zealand into a Free Church theocracy.

It was also in the eighteenth century and the first half of the nineteenth that the great migrations of Highlanders from Scotland added their own distinctive religious elements to the emerging cultures of the new nations overseas. Many of them were Catholics, some Episcopalians and others members of Presbyterian and other Protestant groupings. Where they went and what they did forms a series in several countries abroad of colourful and, from the point of view of the depopulation of the lands they left behind them, tragic episodes.

A favourite of mine amongst the colourful episodes — although it is shot through with sadness — was noted by R B Cunninghame Graham during his adventures in South America in the 1870s. 'Don Roberto' discovered in an outlying settlement of Buenos Aires in Argentina descendants of Scots from Inverness-shire. Their names

Robert Cunninghame Graham, traveller, adventurer, founder with Keir Hardie of the Scottish Labour Party. (National Portrait Gallery London)

were Highland but they were pronounced in the Spanish manner: Camerón, McIntyré, McLeán, Fergusón. They had no knowledge of English and spoke Spanish, in which some of them had set a few words of Gaelic. Most of them, according to Cunninghame Graham, 'had left their glens after Culloden'; and four generations overseas had stripped them of much of their Highland heritage. In the 1870s, they were 'all dark, tall, sinewy men', gauchos, 'riders before the Lord', descendants of Catholic refugees from Scotland after the Forty-Five. This episode demonstrates that the Scots, like other settlers overseas, sometimes took more from than they gave to the local culture in which they ultimately found themselves: that they sometimes became assimilated into these cultures rather than the active agents of the acculturation of other peoples.

A wandering group of Episcopalian Scots, many although not all of whom were of Highland origin, added to the religious complexities of the overseas settlements of the eighteenth and early nineteenth centuries. Loyal to the House of Stewart, many of them sought refuge in the New World. Typical of the Scottish Episcopalian influence overseas were the first Bishops of the Church of England and of the Episcopal Church in Nova Scotia and in the United States, respectively, after the American Revolution. Charles Inglis, who became Anglican Bishop of Nova Scotia in 1787, was the great grandson of a Scottish Episcopal clergyman who had left Glasgow in 1690 and became a wanderer between the Old World and the New, and between the British and American colonies north and south of the Saint Lawrence River. Samuel Seabury, the first American Episcopal Bishop, was obliged to seek consecration in a private chapel in Aberdeen in 1784, because the United States was not under the jurisdiction of the Crown. Like Charles Inglis, he was a man of strong conservative principles and had written influential tracts against the idependence of the American colonies. As a medical student at the University of Edinburgh, where he graduated in 1753, he had worshipped at Old St Paul's Church, Edinburgh, and it was perhaps here that he imbibed his Tory and High Church sympathies.

These men were influenced by the reaction in Scotland against the thorough-going nature of the Reformation north of the Tweed. But there were others, in many parts of the world, who were influenced by the tendency of Protestantism in Scotland to split into sects far beyond the bounds of the doctrine and authority of Presbyterianism. The major Scottish contribution to the development of religion around the world has obviously been the dispersal of Presbyterianism but Scots have also played no small part in the dissemination of several forms of religious sectarianism, some of them highly idiosyncratic. This tendency, implicit in the forces unleashed by the Reformation, especially in its Scottish form, led some on to the rejection of all forms of religious authority. It has been truly said that 'the best effect of the Scotsman's religious training was teaching him to do without his religion'. It enabled him to survive as a certain sort of freethinker: one who, unlike his more familiar fellows, is not so intoxicated with freedom as to forget to think.

The story is instructive here of the family of Andrew Carnegie, for many the supreme embodiment of the Scot abroad, the personification of what Max Weber called 'the Protestant Ethic and the spirit of capitalism'. Carnegie's father, William, broke with his Local Presbyterian Church, itself a product of the Erskine Secessionist movement, on the Sunday after Andrew's birth on the 25th

Andrew Carnegie, who made his fortune in the United States of America and used much of it to further education and cultural improvement. Many of Scotland's public libraries began life as Carnegie Libraries. (Courtesy of the Andrew Carnegie Birthplace)

November 1835 in a highly emotional reaction to the minister's sermon on infant damnation. William Carnegie sought solace in Swedenborgianism; and it was to a Swedenborgian Church that Andrew Carnegie was taken as a boy when the family emigrated to America. He himself ultimately moved right over to the agnostic position. When fame and fortune came to him, he was proud of his membership in the so-called Nineteenth Century Club of New York, an association of American intellectuals who were strongly attracted by the Positivist ideas of Auguste Comte. A lively member of this club was Robert G Ingersoll, the American crusader for free thought at home and abroad in the late nineteenth century; it is possibly significant for the story of the dissemination of humanism as well as religion by Scots into many parts of the world that Ingersoll wrote a poem celebrating the humanity of Robert Burns, a copy of which is displayed in the cottage in Alloway in which Burns was born, although many visitors to what has become almost a sacred shrine of Scotland have never heard of Ingersoll and his gospel of agnosticism. They may, however, have heard of Andrew Carnegie and his gospel of wealth, for he published in 1889 an essay with this as its title. It encouraged the promotion of education, through well-endowed popular libraries and the spread of higher education, especially that with a practical, scientific and technical bias.

When Andrew Carnegie made his celebrated educational endowments, he worked, whether he knew it or not, within the tradition of what Dr George Davie has called 'the democratic intellect', itself a product of the emphasis on education within the Scottish Reformation. By the second half of the eighteenth century and lasting until at least the first quarter of the nineteenth, this produced the remarkable concatenation of great and seminal writers, philosophers and scientists (Adam Smith, David Hume, William Robertson, Walter Scott, Hugh Blair, Joseph Black, James Hutton, James Watt, Adam Ferguson, Thomas Reid, Dugald Stewart, to name only a few of them) that has come to be known as the Scottish Enlightenment. The dispersal of learning from Scotland operated not only at the university level. Scots took abroad or sent abroad the products and patterns of their schools and colleges as well as of their universities. They went to the English-speaking world overseas and also to Asia and Africa where, through the transplanting of their educational institutions and the enterprise of earnest individuals in search of truth, opportunities for social service, and reputation, they made notable contributions to science, pure and applied, to engineering and technology, to the humanities and to the arts. Many of them went overseas ready to extend to others the benefits of the egalitarian, practical kind of education which they themselves had received. Such men were Norman Leys and W McGregor Ross, the one a medical man and the other a railway builder, who pioneered the extension of democracy and education in East and Central Africa in the early twentieth century. Both of them came from a middle-class Scottish background. Norman Leys had been raised by his grandfather, a Lanarkshire Presbyterian minister, who had sworn in a law court that his objective was to imbue the boy with 'the principles of Evangelical truth'. McGregor Ross was the son of a headmaster in Southport, a Gaelic scholar originally from Ross-shire. Neither Leys nor Ross was educated in a public school. As undergraduates, they had received practical training. Ross scoffed at the English disregard for training, so evident in Kenya (where he was working) and praised the general standard of education in 'more enlightened countries — such as Scotland'. 'As Scots', comments Diana Wylie, a perceptive American student of these two Caledonian colonial reformers, 'they disapproved of the English class system and hoped that education would help to dissolve it in Africa as in Britain'.

Scottish publishing houses such as Blackwoods, Chambers' and Nelson's were a cultural comcomitant for those Scots abroad who were determined to spread the benefits of the kind of education which they had received at home. These publishing houses helped them through issuing, often at very popular prices which makes us envious today, original works of literature and scholarship, reprints of established classics, *haute vulgarisation,* and through the popularisation of what used to be called in the nineteenth century 'useful knowledge'. The Scots were great makers of dictionaries in many languages and of handbooks in all subjects, as well as encyclopaedias, from the pioneering days of the first *Encyclopaedia Britannica,* which was issued from Edinburgh in weekly numbers at sixpence a copy between 1768 and 1771. In these ways, in the eighteenth and nineteenth centuries, the Scots, at home and abroad, without government subsidy, anticipated many of the techniques of the Open University.

Scotland, from ancient times to the Union and beyond, has been a land of several languages; and Scots, in their continual moving to different parts of their own country and into England and further afield, gained a degree of linguistic sophistication which their English cousins south of the Border often lacked. Against a background of linguistic variety, co-existing and interacting with the serious attention which Scots paid to academic matters, it is hardly surprising that, in the expansion of the British Empire, Scots made many valuable contributions to the study of non-European languages. I think here, for example, from personal experience, of the work of Scots in the reduction to writing and the analysis of Central African languages. No doubt, they frequently made mistakes, and modern African nationalists do not hesitate to point these out. But Scottish work upon these languages, I believe, will be appreciated by Central Africans in the future. It will be seen as an important contribution to the growth of modern government and ways of life in these countries; and Scottish work on the translations of the Scriptures should be appreciated as an addition to their religious experience.

The Scottish tradition of liberty has gone through many forms since the Declaration of Arbroath in 1320, particularly during the period of the American and French Revolutions, and since the special Scottish interpretation of socialism from the days of Chartism to the Revolt on the Clyde and beyond. Through their writings, their oratory and their transmission, as emigrants, of many-sided ideas of liberty overseas, Scots have made a unique contribution to the theory and practice of human freedom, individual and social. But there are other ways in which Scots have increased the liberty of human beings. Freedom of movement has been increased by vital Scottish contributions to, for example, the development of the steam-engine. And, above all, human suffering has been lightened for many men and women by Scottish men of science such as Sir James Young Simpson, through his discovery of the utility of chloroform as an anaesthetic, and Sir Alexander Fleming by his work on the healing properties of penicillin.

All these things and many more have gone overseas from Scotland, accompanied or unaccompanied. But has it been altogether a one-way process, an outgoing venture? It is relatively easy, in spite of all the historical research which remains to be done, to chart the main

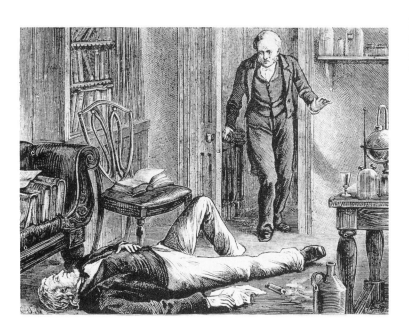

James Young Simpson, experimenting with chloroform, 1847. Six years later chloroform was given to Queen Victoria in childbirth. (Courtesy of the Mansell Collection)

movements of people, practices, institutions and ideas from Scotland to places beyond its borders. It is less easy, however, with the exception perhaps of English and Irish influences on Scotland, to estimate what the experience of foreign elements has meant for Scotland. But one thing seems likely: over several centuries, and particularly since 1707, both emigration abroad and the introduction of foreign elements into its midst have strengthened the sense of Scottish nationality. It could, of course, be argued that the loss of large numbers of people, during a long period of closeness to a dominant political and economic rival, partner, master — whichever term you prefer — dilutes national feeling. But I doubt if this is so. Certainly, one of the most travelled of nineteenth century Scots, Robert Louis Stevenson, would not have agreed. At the front of his *Memories and Portraits,* first published in 1887, in his discerning essay 'The Foreigner at Home', he bore witness to the manner in which travel outside of Scotland strengthened the consciousness of Scottish identity. 'A Scotchman,' he declared, 'may tramp the better part of Europe and the United States, and never again receive so vivid an impression of foreign travel and strange lands and manners as his first excursion into England.' Further afield, he gave two other examples of this process at work. 'When the Black Watch,' said Stevenson, 'after many years of foreign service, returned to Scotland, veterans leaped out and kissed the earth at Port Patrick.' It is a common axiom in the study of nationalism in general that a period of residence outside of one's country of birth strengthens national feeling. This process seems to have been particularly strong with Scots, excellent settlers though they usually were and ready to come to terms with local societies and cultures.

It is abundantly evident that Scotland, in spite of its smallness, geographically and demographically, played a part in the creation of the modern world out of all proportion to its size. As one examines the many aspects of this, one is inclined to put them all on the credit side. But are there no debit entries? And if there are, is one doing a service to the appreciation of Scottish activities abroad by concealing them?

There are, I would tentatively suggest, at least three debit entries. The first, it could be argued, is that Scottish settlements and Scottish influences abroad were masculine-dominated. Until very much more work has been done, the place of women in Scottish activities abroad is not easy to describe or to value. Looking over the two and a half centuries since 1707 and, particularly, at the eighteenth century and the first half of the nineteenth when so much of the characteristic pattern of Scottish influences abroad was established, the feminine element is noted for its anonymity in most, if not all, of the historical writings at present at our disposal. There are a few outstanding female names; but they figure in most of the published accounts largely, it seems, for romantic reasons. Foremost amongst them is Flora MacDonald, that gallant woman who, after sterling service to Prince Charles Edward Stuart, accompanied her husband, Captain Allan MacDonald of Kingburg, to North Carolina, stuck to him through thick and thin, and then came home again to Scotland with him, after he had backed George III and the losing side in the American War of Independence.

Occasionally, the name of a Scottish woman abroad who identified herself entirely with her husband's interests and was responsible for many of his successes has been preserved for posterity. The

Elsie Inglis, physician, surgeon and campaigner for women's suffrage. In the First World War she joined the Serbs in their resistance to German and Austrian invasion. In this photograph she is in Serbian uniform. (Courtesy of the Elsie Inglis Memorial Maternity Hospital)

outstanding name here is probably that of the long-suffering Mary Moffat, wife of David Livingstone, who died so pathetically on the Zambesi in 1862 at the age of forty-one. But such women, in the complex story of the Scottish Diaspora, are too often taken for granted.

By the end of the nineteenth century, a new type of Scottish woman abroad was coming to be noticed. The trail had been blazed by Dundee-born Frances Wright (1795-1852), freethinker and secularist crusader, who visited the United States on several occasions; wrote important books and pamphlets about them; set up a community for freed slaves in Tennessee; helped Robert Dale Owen to edit *The New Harmony-Gazette,* a utopian socialist periodical; and lectured to large American audiences on women's rights, free education, birth control, equitable distribution of wealth, and the errors of organised religion. At the start of the twentieth century, the increasing emergence of this independent type of Scottish woman, intent upon making her own contribution to the Scottish Diaspora, was revealed in the services for suffering humanity by two other women from Scotland: Mary Slessor, a mill-worker from Dundee, whose missionary labours under the auspices of the United Presbyterian Church at Calabar in Nigeria between 1876 and 1915 are still remembered with affection and gratitude by many West Africans; and Dr Elsie Inglis, descendant of Highlanders who had worked in such different parts of the world as South Carolina and India, where she was born in 1864 and from where she went on to gain medical qualifications and to give devoted service in hospitals in Scotland and overseas, particularly during the First World War. As Dame Rebecca West, a former pupil of George Watson's Ladies College in Edinburgh and herself an outstanding example of the independent female on the Scottish Diaspora, said of Dr Elsie Inglis in her great book on Jugoslavia, *Black Lamb and Grey Falcon,* 'Dr Elsie Inglis' Scottish Women's Hospital [amongst the wartime Serbs] left an imperishably glorious name'.

But such women were exceptions. Would it be unkind, would it be inaccurate, to say that this great wave of transplanted men, women and children was dominated by males and by the image of masculinity in Scotland, of Scottish *machismo?* It is Scottish *machismo,* some would claim, which was responsible for the second debit entry in the accounts of Scotland's mark on the world: the abuse of alcohol, especially of whisky. In this respect, I am reminded of two contrasting pictures of a typical and valuable Scottish contributor to the extension of communications across the world: the ship's engineer. On the one hand, there is Rudyard Kipling's righteous creation in his poem 'McAndrew's Hymn', of 1893: 'Predestination in the stride o' yon connectin'-rod . . . Be thanks to Thee Most High!' On the other hand, we have Will Fyffe's far less respectable figure of the 1930s variety theatres, the drunken ship's engineer, to whom Glasgow belonged when he had had two drinks on a Saturday!

And a third possible debit entry could be attributed to the ethnocentrism of some Scots abroad. We have already noted Professor Dewar Gibb's comment on the seventeenth century Scotch-Irish: 'They were of a superior race and they meant to keep that race pure.' Three hundred years later, one of their descendants in North Carolina, the Reverend Thomas Dixon, Junior, author of the novel glorifying the work of the Ku Klux Klan after the American Civil War, entitled *The Clansman* and originally published in 1905, on which D W Griffith based the first massive modern movie, *The Birth of a Nation,* at the beginning of his book referred with rapture to 'the fiery cross of old Scotland's hills' and described the Ku Klux Klanners as 're-incarnated souls of the Clansman of Old Scotland'. And it deserves to be noted here that the first supposedly scientific work on race in modern times, which put the Caucasians at the top of the scale and the Blacks at the bottom, was by a Scottish doctor who had served in the Kaffir Wars in South Africa: Robert Knox, the Edinburgh anatomist, whose book, *The Races of Men,* was published in 1850.

Some might be inclined to add a fourth debit entry at this stage: the tendency of Scottish culture, especially when far away from home, to assume an unduly sentimental form, continually looking homeward and cultivating, often to a maudlin extent, the kailyards of the ancestral spirits. But sentiment, however disproportionate it may be at times, is at least human feeling; and it would surely be inconsiderate to accuse the Scots of taking human feelings overseas with them, would it not? And, at the religious level, the words of G K Chesterton may help to put this problem into perspective. 'It might be said', declared Chesterton, 'that among the Scots, so far from a sentimental religiosity taking the place of dogmatic religion (as is generally the case among the English), something like the very opposite . . . [has] occurred. When the religion was dead, the theology remained; at any rate, the taste for theology remained. It remained. because, whatever else it is, theology is at least a form of thought.'

However many debit entries one is inclined to put into the account of the Scots in world perspective, in my opinion the books balance and the account is well in credit. At a time when the great age of migration is over for Scots, as for all other white men, and when the non-white races of humanity are coming increasingly to the front in world history, an accumulation of spiritual capital remains in it, upon which the people of Scotland can draw for themselves and for others in the fearsome future which confronts us all.

*The fame of David Livingstone, as missionary, doctor and
explorer in Africa, was worldwide. Here, he is with his wife
Mary and their family at Lake Ngami in 1850. Livingstone
was one of the many individuals who sent material to the
newly-founded Museum in Edinburgh, which attracted
donations from Scots all over the world. With such support the
new Museum flourished.*

*A strong campaigner for the foundation of a national museum
for Scotland was Professor Robert Jameson, a leading light in
natural history and geological studies for half a century.*

A SOURCE OF INSPIRATION: ROBERT JAMESON

Jenni Calder and S M Andrews

In 1817 Robert Jameson, Professor of Natural History at Edinburgh University, drew up instructions for potential collectors of material for the University's Natural History Museum. The instructions covered every aspect of the natural world, plants and minerals as well as animal life, and gave details on means of preserving and packing specimens.

> Quadrupeds and birds to be preserved by taking off their skins, which may easily be done, by making an incision in a straight line, from the vent to the throat, and removing the skin by means of a blunt knife. The skull and bones of the legs and feet to be left.

A recipe for the preservation of skins was provided. Reptiles and fish were 'best preserved in a spirit of wine, rum, or whisky'. Minerals were to be wrapped in layers of gauze, cotton and paper. The mineral collector should be armed with hammers, chisels, boring-irons, a compass, a goniometer (an instrument for measuring angles), magnifying glass and blow-pipe.

Professor Jameson was a collector, and he had a vision of hundreds more keen collectors all over the world equipped to gather the raw materials of natural science, to ensure continuing achievement in its study at Edinburgh.

Jameson, the son of a Leith soap manufacturer, held the Natural History Chair for half a century from 1804. Edinburgh's great Enlightenment period had helped to generate a spirit of enquiry in Scotland that remained powerful. Jameson was a dominating and a controversial figure in two burgeoning areas of science, zoology and geology. There is no doubt that his work and reputation were partly fuelled by the rapid growth of these sciences and by their increasing popularity, but as we shall see this is not the whole story. The zoological description and identification of new species had been going on for a long time, but enquiry was intensified as far-flung parts of the world and their wildlife became accessible. In the early years of the nineteenth century geology was still very young, and its study was carried forward by a great wave of enthusiasm, much of it amateur. Jameson was one of a number of notable figures who encouraged and co-ordinated this, contributing to the debate raging at that time on the origin of the structure of the earth. There were then two rival theories: one (called Neptunism) propounded by Abraham Werner, under whom Jameson had studied at Freiburg, and the other (Plutonism) put forward by James Hutton in Edinburgh, a few years before Jameson took up his Chair. Jameson adamantly adhered to the theory of his mentor, perpetuating the debate in Edinburgh long after it had subsided elsewhere.

Edinburgh was one of the few places in the world where a wide-ranging study of natural history could be made, and under Jameson its reputation grew. He himself taught both mineralogy and zoology, though his main enthusiasm was for the former. He founded the

Robert Jameson, Professor of Natural History at Edinburgh University from 1804 to 1854, and mastermind of natural science collecting.

Wernerian Natural History Society, which flourished for many years. His classes were packed. Medical students formed a high proportion of those attending, but many others also signed on from their particular interest in an emerging science. Instruction was not confined to the classroom. The Edinburgh area was a rich source of geological evidence, and Jameson led his classes on field excursions. He would cheerfully and energetically spend a day out on the hills, exhausting his followers, returning home as vigorous as when he set out. His energy and enthusiasm clearly made a great impression on his students, although it was not so much that Jameson was a riveting lecturer; on the contrary, there was much criticism of his style. Thomas Carlyle as a student was not at all impressed, and grumbled about Jameson's presentation of a 'chaos of facts'. The young Darwin, also at Edinburgh University, found him 'incredibly dull'. In spite of this, Jameson exerted a powerful and productive influence on a large number of individuals, who carried the study of natural history far and wide.

There are many accounts of his genial and encouraging attitude towards those who agreed with his theory. Amongst the men with whom he developed a mutually rewarding relationship was William Scoresby, an English whaler who spent some time in Edinburgh and attended Jameson's classes. Jameson, interested in this young man who not only had an avid interest in the natural world but recorded his observations during whaling trips to the Arctic, often invited Scoresby to his home. Scoresby felt out of place at first, embarrassed by his humble origins and rough trade, but Jameson's kindness soon dispelled this. Scoresby would go on to be of considerable use to him, sending material from the Arctic, including a live polar bear. The beast was lodged in a 'commodious den' at the University. Another live resident of the Museum was a playful puma sent to Jameson in 1826 by Lord Napier, captain of the frigate *Diamond* which brought back from South America both live and dead specimens for the University.

It was not only students who fell under Jameson's spell. When the American naturalist and artist Audubon visited Edinburgh in 1826 he met Jameson, whom he ranked in significance with Sir Walter Scott, and found him keen and cordial, and 'full of the nobleness which comes from a kind, generous heart'. It was of course to Jameson's advantage to develop good relations with fellow naturalists and geologists, for many could be useful to his department and his collection. Jameson did not hesitate to ask bluntly for what he wanted, as another letter to Scoresby illustrates.

As naturalists are great beggars I have to request of you as a particular favour to endeavour to procure for me the head of a sea unicorn [narwhal] — and also of the saw fish and if you could add to these the head of a horse [sea horse or walrus] and two or three sealskulls it would be increasing the obligation tenfold. You know I long much for the skins of some of the Greenland birds, particularly the fulmar. I would also take the liberty of directing your attention to the finny turtle?

Jameson not only took advantage of every possible contact to encourage collecting. He actively enlisted the assistance and support of government. He approached Lord Melville of the Admiralty to ask for material brought back by expeditions to the Arctic. And it was with the official approval of Lord Castlereagh, the Foreign Secretary, that Jameson's Instructions of 1817 were distributed to 'ministers and public servants abroad'. Copies of Jameson's Instructions were put into the hands of missionaries and doctors, army and navy personnel and colonial administrators in Africa and the East, the Americas and the Pacific. Some of those who were armed with these Instructions had been to Jameson's classes, but many others would have had little direct acquaintance with zoological or geological material. Even for the knowledgeable amateur a certain amount of dedication was required to fulfil Jameson's requirements.

The professional naturalist, like the professional geologist, was still a rarity. The idea of becoming a professional scientist was very new, and those who did were mainly well-to-do academics. Science in the early nineteenth century was a vocation rather than a career. The combining of medicine with the pursuit of natural science became increasingly common. Two of Scotland's most notable surgeon/naturalists, both associated with Jameson, were Sir Andrew Smith and Sir John Richardson. Both were explorers and collectors,

Mauritius Blue Pigeon,
part of the collection of
Louis Dufresne of the
Museum d'Histoire
Naturelle in Paris,
acquired by Jameson in
1819 after considerable
negotiation. (NMS)

A tortoise collected and described by Sir Andrew Smith, an Edinburgh trained army surgeon posted to Cape Town. Smith sent important material to the Museum in Edinburgh, thus continuing the tradition established by Robert Jameson. (NMS)

both made significant contributions to science, and both had distinguished careers in medicine. The early decades of the nineteenth century saw Britain taking a lead in exploration, and in this Scots played a prominent and often initiatory role. On expeditions a surgeon was a necessity. His value was double if he combined his medical duties with collecting important evidence of the environment and the life it sustained.

Many of those fired by Jameson's zeal combined an involvement in science with rather different kinds of activity. It was through the offices of Lieutenant-Colonel Patrick Lindsay, a friend of Jameson born in Musselburgh, that material collected on Captain Sturt's 1828 expedition into the interior of south-east Australia was sent to Edinburgh. Jameson described Lindsay as 'a very active naturalist', but he made the army his career. Major General Lord Greenock, who became Governor of Edinburgh Castle in 1837, also attended Jameson's lectures and devoted much of his spare time to collecting geological specimens.

Scotland was an exciting place to be for the geologist at this time, for discoveries were being made of fossil material which contributed to theories that the world was many millions of years older than had once been unquestioningly assumed. Geological interest had focused on Scotland not only through the material to be found there but through the individuals who were making the discoveries and generating new ideas. The work of James Hutton, whose *Theory of the Earth* was published in 1795, had established Edinburgh as a

Sturt's Overland Expedition leaving Adelaide, 10th August, 1844. S T Gill. Material collected on this expedition was sent to Edinburgh. (Art Gallery of South Australia, Adelaide)

centre of geological enquiry. John Walker, Jameson's predecessor as Professor of Natural History, was also a mineralogist and continued this tradition, as did Jameson himself and the many geologists associated with him, although contesting Hutton's theory. The debate about the origin and formation of the earth's structure developed into a battle that shook Edinburgh society, in which Jameson and his party were vanquished. 'Though I don't care for geology,' commented John Gibson Lockhart, 'I do like to see the fellows fight.'

Jameson was truculent in defeat, and was always hostile towards those of Huttonian views who wished to make use of the University's geology collections. Hutton's own specimens were among these, but Jameson neglected them and allowed them to be lost. This attitude produced a growing number of opponents who voiced strong and bitter criticisms of him during the 1826 Royal Commission on Scottish Universities.

Jameson's achievement, however, did not rest on his contribution to geological theory, but on the way he inspired so many to become naturalists and collect and return material to Edinburgh's Natural History Museum, whose value increased and was widely acknowledged. The collections were used by Jameson for teaching purposes, and it was perhaps the direct contact with this material that encouraged his ex-students to look for more. His lectures may have been dry, his approach intellectually dogmatic, but there was commitment, dedication, an eagerness in investigation, a total conviction that he was engaged in a vital study, and all this was communicated. Jameson was a magnetic force that attracted material from every continent. With the aid of this material he furthered the study of natural science and commanded international respect.

Although a teaching collection, the Natural History Museum was also open to the public on payment of an admission charge of half-a-crown. Jameson became increasingly preoccupied with the need to make the material more accessible to the public. As the collections expanded the need for more space became desperate. But Jameson wanted not only more spacious accommodation for the Museum in which he was accused of taking too possessive an interest; he wanted it to become 'a public department connected in some degree with the country of Scotland; it is the National Museum of this country'. In talking of a national museum for Scotland Jameson was a quarter of a century before his time. There was in 1826, when these words were recorded, only one national museum, the British Museum in London, and access to that was not easy. Jameson himself had some difficulty in obtaining a ticket when he visited London as a young man. Now he wanted the natural history material that he had been largely responsible for gathering together to be available to the Scottish public.

This would happen eventually, but sadly Jameson died in the very year, 1854, that a new museum was created for Scotland. Within the collections of that museum, now the Royal Museum of Scotland, there still survives the evidence of the enterprise of Jameson and his many associates.

*In Robert Jameson's time Edinburgh University's Natural
History Museum was housed in premises (above) in what is
now the Old College. The first university zoological
collections were initiated in the 17th century by Robert
Sibbald and Andrew Balfour.
By the 19th century many Scots abroad had a keen interest in
natural science, and some collected important material that
was new to science. One of these collectors was Robert Neill.*

ROBERT NEILL: ARTIST AND NATURALIST

Geoffrey N Swinney

'The people are a strange set never easy but when in hot water full of gossip and like all little dirty places the only way is to be intimate with no one, and I believe I am the only exception among the motely group of its inhabitants who can say there is not a man in it, from the Resident down to the Sergeant that I am not on good terms with — we never give tea parties they lead to lead bullets in dirty little holes — I have dined out 8 or 10 times and only at Lady Spencers or the Residents, they don't expect us to give returns so it is alright . . .

Deputy Assistant Commissary General Robert Neill was describing the Western Australian township of Albany in a letter, dated April 1942, to his friend Thomas Scott. The port, situated on the sheltered deep-water anchorage of King George's Sound, was used mainly by whalers working the rich Southern Ocean, and by vessels on passage to New South Wales and Van Diemens Land. It was a rough place and clearly not a pleasant posting.

The town had been established as a penal settlement in 1826, but after only four years all but one of the convicts were removed and the area opened to free settlement. But conditions in Western Australia in the early 1830s were not conducive to settlers and the town grew only slowly.

In March 1836 the *Beagle* put in to the Sound to reprovision. Charles Darwin later recalled the visit: 'I do not remember, since leaving England, having passed a more dull and uninteresting time.' Darwin was at King George's Sound nine days: Robert Neill was to be there almost nine years.

When Neill arrived at Albany in 1839 the total population numbered 156, 23 of whom were Scots. As the officer in charge of the commissariat stores he had a responsible position in the small community. Soon he was appointed District Officer for the Western Australian Bank and made a magistrate. Despite this, Neill was something of a loner and kept himself aloof from his fellow townsfolk. Having a post in the Commissariat which provided him sufficient leisure time, Robert Neill withdrew into his hobby — sketching and painting. He had always been a keen artist, sketching the people and places around him, both at King George's Sound and before that whilst stationed in Tasmania. Those of his drawings which have been preserved provide a tantalising glimpse of life in the early settlements of southern Australia.

Neill's story may be seen as a case study, of one of the many who, in the years of depression that followed the Napoleonic Wars, left their native Scotland to seek a new life in the colonies. Robert Neill's father, James, had been a partner in the family printing business Neill & Co in Edinburgh. The purchase of a farm on the outskirts of the city in 1808 led to James incurring substantial debts. The use of the firm's funds to help pay off his creditors caused a dispute between

James and his cousin and business partner, Patrick Neill, which resulted in the break up of the family business. For a while James and Patrick ran rival printing shops in adjoining premises in Edinburgh's Fishmarket Close, but in 1820 James quit Scotland. He sailed together with his wife and their three children, James, Robert and Ann, aboard the *Skelton* and docked in Hobart, Tasmania on 27th November, 1820.

Within a few weeks of their arrival both sons had gained employment in the Commissariat Department. Robert, then nineteen, was appointed a temporary clerk, a post which paid two shillings and sixpence a day but which carried with it a grant of 200 acres of land at Macquarie Plains. For six years Robert worked in Hobart and in the years 1823-6 had charge of both H M Magazine and Bonding Warehouse. By 1826 his salary had risen to seven shillings and sixpence per day. In that year he was gazetted Assistant Surveyor of Lands, at a salary of £300 per annum, but was prevented from taking up the position.

An interest in natural history seems to have been a characteristic of the Neill family. Patrick Neill, Robert's first cousin once removed, was the most eminent naturalist of the family, being for many years the secretary to Edinburgh's Wernerian Society. James Neill Snr too had a keen interest in the subject. An obituary in the Hobart Town Courier described James as:

> . . . a gentleman of very enlarged mind, richly stored with scientific knowledge, more especially in natural history, to the cultivation of which in this island he devoted much attention during the latter years of his life.

Robert clearly inherited this interest, for in 1824, in collaboration with a Dr Spence, he made a collection of Tasmanian plants. This collection is now in the herbarium of the Royal Botanic Garden, Edinburgh.

Almost as soon as he had arrived in Tasmania, Robert Neill began sketching. One of his earliest studies of aborigines, drawn in 1821, is in the Mitchell Library, Sydney, along with two other studies dated January 1828. One of these was the basis of the engraving *Indigènes des Deux Sèxes (Van Diemen)* published in *Voyage de la Corvette L'Astolabe:* the French expedition having been in Hobart during December 1827 and January 1828. In 1829 he became involved in an ill-fated forerunner of what was to become one of Tasmania's major industries. The Edinburgh Horticultural Society's transactions record the enterprise:

> The seedling apples raised by Mr D Stanfield, of Clarence Plains, had been transmitted to the Committee early in September; one of these apples was a foot in circumference, and of beautiful appearance, but the specimens having been plucked on 15th April last, and having passed through the tropics, were too much decayed to afford a correct estimate of their flavour. Thanks were voted to Mr Robert Neill of the Commissariat Office, Hobart Town, who transmitted these fruits.

Robert continued to paint and sketch following his posting, in 1831, to the penal settlement at Darlington on Maria Island. His paintings provided us with some of the earliest pictorial records of the settlement. Three still survive, one in the Queen Victoria Museum in Launceston, Tasmania and the others in private hands. It was probably about this time that he produced the small oval painting *The Natives of Van Diemen's Land,* which illustrated Ross's

The penal settlement at Darlington, Maria Island, Tasmania painted by Robert Neill. In a private collection in Sydney. (Geoffrey N Swinney)

Hobart Town Almanack for 1830, the original of which is held by the National Library of Australia.

By 1833 Robert had been transferred from Maria Island to the large penal colony at Port Arthur. George Augustus Robinson records in his journal a visit to that settlement on St Patrick's Day, 1833:

> . . . received an invitation from Mr Neill the commissariat storekeeper to take tea . . . Mr Neill is an artist: presented me with a portrait of Truggernann a female aborigine of VDL taken in 1828. This was very acceptable to me.

Unfortunately, this portrait does not seem to have survived but an engraving based on a small sketch by Robert Neill of a Cape Barren Goose, dated July 1830, once in the possession of Robinson, is now in the Museum of Mankind, London. This sketch, another in a letter to Thomas Lemprière and three contained in Thomas Scott's notebook, both manuscripts in the Mitchell Library, appear to be the only other of Neill's drawings surviving from his years in Tasmania.

Soon after Robinson's visit Neill was recalled to Hobart, where he met Helen Storey. They were married on 13th November 1834 at St David's Church and bought a house in Campbell Street, where they lived until 1836 when Robert was transferred to Launceston. The journey to Launceston was not particularly pleasant for the couple, who by now had a young daughter less than a year old. In a letter to Lemprière, who had succeeded him at Port Arthur, Robert described the trip: 'After five days of jolting in the caravan called Cutt's Conveyance and having had tolerably good weather with diverse narrow escapes from an upset we all got safe and sound'. In January 1837 both Neill and Lemprière were promoted to the rank of Deputy Assistant Commissary General. In August of that same year Thomas Lemprière had an interview with their commanding officer. He recorded the outcome in his diary: 'Called on Mr Moodie — he decided nothing except that Neill should go to King George's Sound instead of me'. So it was that on 12th August, 1839 Robert and Helen Neill and their family, took passage for Albany aboard the *Fox*.

As officer in charge of the stores Robert Neill would have been responsible for the bi-monthly issue of flour made to the 280 or so aborigines in the area. They were subjects for his sketches, two of which he sent to his sister, who by 1842 had returned to Edinburgh. These drawings were later used as the basis for illustrations in R Brough Smyth's book *The Aborigines of Victoria*. In 1841, Neill set about combining his artistic skills with his interest in natural history, by making a collection of the animals to be found in the area of King George's Sound. He collected mainly fishes, which either he caught himself or were given to him by the local aborigines. Knowing that the colours of preserved fishes fade, he recorded the colours and patterns of many of his specimens in the form of life-size watercolour paintings. In addition he kept detailed notes on the habits of each species.

Robert Neill was in the process of amassing his collection when in July 1841 Edward John Eyre and his faithful aboriginal companion

Letter from Neill to his sister Ann in Edinburgh, containing sketches of Australian aborigines on which were based illustrations for R Brough Smyth's *Aborigines of Victoria*, 1878. (Courtesy of Sir John Clerk of Penicuik)

Wylie tramped wearily into Albany. Eyre had set out from Adelaide some ten months earlier in an attempt to pioneer an overland route to the growing settlements of Western Australia. The expedition had met with disaster: one of his group had been murdered, all but one of his aborigines had deserted and after incredible hardship only Eyre and Wylie completed the trek. Neill sketched the arrival of the wretched pair in Albany. This picture together with another couple of his watercolours were used as the basis for illustrations in Eyre's *Journals of Expeditions of Discovery*.

Eyre's had been primarily a journey of discovery, not a scientific expedition. But it was probably the lack of scientific material from the expedition that prompted Robert to show his fish paintings to a former Government Resident at Albany, Captain George Grey. By 1841 Grey was Governor of South Australia. It was Governor Grey who persuaded Neill to send his paintings and notes to London. The folio of fifty-eight watercolours of fish, eight of reptiles and one of a small mammal was duly despatched and is now in the Zoology Library of the British Museum (Natural History). It was examined by two of the foremost biologists of their day, John Edward Gray and Sir John Richardson. These two eminent men of science edited Neill's notes and published them as an appendix to Eyre's narrative of his expedition. Unfortunately, the paintings themselves were never published.

In 1848 Robert Neill, now promoted Assistant Commissary General, was recalled to Britain. Life in Western Australia had been harsh and dysentery had claimed the lives of several of his children. He longed for a posting to a more pleasant situation:

> . . . this is a horrid isolated place the most expensive perhaps in the world . . . were I to wish for a station the Cape of Good Hope of all places would be the place — you can live cheaper there than anywhere else and the climate is good.

He spent several months in Britain during which he visited his cousin Patrick and attended various scientific meetings. To some of these he presented the material he had brought back from Australia. These included his fish collection. Sir John Richardson examined this and from it described several species new to science. This small, but important collection was deposited in the museum of the Free Church College in Edinburgh from where it was eventually transferred into what is now the National Museums of Scotland.

Neill eventually got his new posting, not to the Cape, as he had wished, but to the Leeward and Windward Islands, where he arrived in late March 1849. Sadly, the climate in the Caribbean was little more kind to Europeans than that of Western Australia. Robert Neill fell ill with yellow fever and died in Barbados on 30th September 1852. His wife and the rest of his family died in the same epidemic.

The 'Scotchman', as Neill was known in the service, had contributed in several ways to our knowledge of Australia. His collection of plants and particularly his fish collection were of considerable scientific value and his sketches and paintings have left us with a vivid, if fragmentary, pictorial record of life in Australia's frontier settlements. His pictures of aborigines in Tasmania are of especial interest, for they help chronicle a people whose way of life, even in Neill's day, had been disrupted by European settlement. By 1876 they had been exterminated. One of the last Tasmanian aborigines was Trugernanna, the woman Robert Neill had sketched nearly 50 years earlier.

Smellie's printing Office. foot of Anchor Close.

*William Smellie's printing office in Anchor Close, Edinburgh,
was a focus of intellectual life in the 18th century. Smellie
edited and printed the first* Encyclopaedia Britannica *in 1768.
Patrick Neill, cousin of Robert Neill's father whose lack of
success in the trade led to his departure from Scotland, was
another leading printer. He also played an important role in
the scientific community.
The brothers Daniel and George Wilson were of a younger
generation, inheriting the legacy of the Scottish
Enlightenment. They were both major figures in developing
and communicating new areas of science and learning.*

NEW FRONTIERS:
GEORGE AND DANIEL WILSON

Marinell Ash

Daniel and George Wilson were well-known figures in the intellectual circles of mid-nineteenth century Edinburgh. A friend of this period, the historian John Hill Burton, described them:

> Daniel was . . . noticeable among men as tall, wiry and erect. His brother the chemist was small and so sickly and fragile in aspect that one had a nervous feeling, when he was present, as if some fit or worse might befall him: and yet, in company the genial spirit within him shone forth and made him as full of pleasant talk as any Hercules of the table.

Members of their circle included the artists D O Hill, George Harvey and Joseph Noel Paton, the scientist Edward Forbes, the surgeon and experimenter with anaesthesia James Young Simpson, literary and historical scholars such as David Laing and Cosmo Innes, the lawyer and Greek scholar, John Stuart Blackie, and the publishers, William Nelson and Robert Chambers. The Wilsons were members of a remarkable group of men who made the cultural life of Edinburgh in the mid-nineteenth century scarcely less brilliant than that of the period of the Enlightenment. Indeed, the intellectual debt of Daniel and George Wilson to the Scottish social theorists of the eighteenth century was to be a dominating feature of their lives.

Daniel and George Wilson were born in Edinburgh in 1816 and 1818, part of the large family of a not very successful wine merchant. The family home was at the base of the Calton Hill on the fringes of the New Town. The dominant influence on their childhood was their strong-minded and talented mother, Jesse Aitkin, described by their cousin, the novelist Mrs Oliphant, as: 'bright, vivacious . . . a universal devourer of books, with that kind of scientific tendency which made her encourage her numerous children to form museums and collect fossils and butterflies.'

The first museum the brothers formed was in a glass-fronted cabinet donated by their mother. With a group of school friends who called themselves 'The Juvenile Society for the Advancement of Knowledge' they ranged the town and surrounding countryside collecting rocks and other curiosities for their cabinet. The Juvenile Society also published a journal, the first of many edited by Daniel who also designed its monogram, helped by George. It contained accounts of their weekly meetings when questions such as 'Is the camel more useful to the Arab or the reindeer to the Laplander?' were earnestly debated.

The Wilson brothers attended the High School of Edinburgh but a good deal of their real schooling took place in the streets of Edinburgh itself. From an early age Daniel was fascinated by the Old Town. He spent much time exploring and sketching in its decaying medieval wynds and closes. Calton Hill and Arthur's Seat were other favourite places to explore: not only for their old and new buildings

George Wilson, first Director of the Industrial Museum of Scotland and Professor of Technology at Edinburgh University, 1854-9. (National Galleries of Scotland)

but for their flora and their geology.

The Wilson household was a happy, yet serious-minded, one. From an early age the children of the family were imbued with a sense that their talents were not only the key to the future but that they must be used to help society. George showed marked scientific ability and decided that he would be a professor in Edinburgh University — although he was not sure in what field. Daniel was a bit less certain about his future vocation: the multiplicity of his gifts may have made a decision difficult. He left school at the age of fifteen and was apprenticed to the Edinburgh line engraver, William Miller. He also attended classes at Edinburgh University but never matriculated or took a degree. George also left the High School of Edinburgh at the age of fifteen and entered the Royal Infirmary of Edinburgh in 1834 for a four year apprenticeship, although he soon realised that he could never be a working surgeon — the blood and pain he witnessed were too distressing. In 1836-7 he spent eighteen months in the chemistry laboratory of Professor (later Sir) Robert Christison at Edinburgh University. Here George Wilson found his life's work: a clean and logical science that could be applied to improve the lives of his fellow men.

While still in his teens Daniel had fallen in love with Margaret Mackay, the daughter of a Glasgow merchant. In 1837, when he was twenty-one, he left Edinburgh for London to seek a living which would allow him to marry and support a family. He tried his hand at play-writing, submitting a script to the actor-manager, Macready (who was complimentary, but did not produce it). His first major commission was to engrave a painting by J M W Turner, an experience Daniel Wilson later recalled as 'the art of extracting sunbeams from cucumbers'.

Daniel's labours were lightened by the arrival of George late in 1838, who came south in the hopes of meeting his hero, Faraday. Instead he became an assistant to a Professor in London University, and while there met Lyon Playfair and a young Scottish medical student named David Livingstone. The brothers set up bachelor apartments in Euston and spent their spare time exploring the sights of London and the surrounding countryside, and editing yet another private journal, entitled 'Quirks, Quips and Quodlibets by Bottle Imp and Mynheer von Scratch'. The pseudonym chosen by Daniel indicates the changing direction of his life; after his Turner engraving he did little more such work but turned instead to writing, primarily for the many journals that were springing up to meet the growing demand for 'useful information' by the rising middle classes of Britain. By the early 1840s he was regularly writing for magazines such as *Chambers Edinburgh Journal, Tait's Edinburgh Magazine* and *The British Quarterly Review*.

In 1840 Daniel returned to Scotland to wed his 'Maggie', the beginning of nearly half a century of happily married life. In the same year, however, George's life had taken a turning towards tragedy. Although not strong, George was an enthusiastic walker, and in the late summer during the course of a tour near Stirling he had been drenched in a sudden rainstorm, and had also sprained his ankle. By the autumn George was seriously ill, the start of the rheumatism that was to dog the rest of his life. An abscess formed on his sprained ankle that refused to heal.

George had been unable to find full-time employment — his Baptist beliefs meant that he was unwilling to sign the articles accepting the Confession of Faith and Formula of Obedience of the Church of Scotland required to hold a chair in a Scottish University — but in 1840 he was licenced by the College of Surgeons in Edinburgh to lecture in chemistry to their diploma candidates. He set up in rooms and a laboratory in Brown Square, overlooking Greyfriars Kirk. His public lectures were also popular, marked by the clarity with which he could explain difficult scientific concepts and principles to lay audiences. George's research and teaching were, however, punctuated by increasing ill health. At last, late in 1842, it became clear that his foot would have to be amputated.

By the time George underwent his ordeal (his friend, Simpson, had not yet discovered anaesthesia), Daniel had moved back to Edinburgh with his young family and had opened an artists' supply and print shop in the New Town. He continued his journalism and within a few weeks of his return he was working on the sketches for what was to become his first major book, *Memorials of Edinburgh in the Olden Time* (1848): a collection of engravings and histories of the ancient buildings of Edinburgh that were fast-disappearing in the civic improvements of the mid-nineteenth century.

Increasingly Daniel Wilson was drawn towards antiquarian

scholarship. Soon after his return to Edinburgh he had heard of a
medieval baptismal stoup on the ground floor of a powder magazine
in Edinburgh Castle. When he visited the building Daniel Wilson
quickly realised that the stoup was in fact the socket for a Romanes-
que column and that the building was the chapel said to have been
built by Queen Margaret, the saintly wife of Malcolm Canmore,
King of Scots (c 1031-93). Such discoveries brought him to the notice
of Edinburgh antiquaries, such as the literary scholar and Signet
Librarian, David Laing, and led to his election, in 1846, as a Fellow
of the Society of Antiquaries of Scotland.

The Society and its Museum had led a precarious existence since
their foundation in 1780. By the 1830s the Antiquaries' Museum
was housed in the 'Building for the Societies' (now the Royal Scottish
Academy) on the Mound. The Museum was a private collection, but
the Fellows of the Society were much concerned that it should be
open to the public; the 1830s and 40s were the period when
museums of this sort were seen as agents of popular education;
indeed the Scottish Antiquaries felt they had a responsibility for
educating the Scottish people about their total archaeological past,
and not just the artefacts in their own collection. In the late 1820s,
for example the Society, had been active in the campaign for the
return of the fifteenth century cannon, 'Mons Meg', to Edinburgh.
By the 1840s, however, the Antiquaries' increasingly perilous financial position was limiting the scope of their activities. They had fallen
into arrears of rent for the apartments, and the Government was
threatening to sell their collection to recover the money owed to
them.

Daniel Wilson entered the Society of Antiquaries just at the time
that the crisis over the future of the Society and its Museum was
reaching a climax. He and David Laing joined forces in a hard-
fought, and ultimately successful, campaign to persuade the Government to take over the Society's collection as the basis of a national
'Museum of Scottish Antiquities'. They saw the campaign to save the
Museum as just one part of a wider campaign to make Scots aware of
their archaeological and historical heritage which was increasingly
threatened by civic improvements, industrial development and railway building. In the later 1840s — largely due to Daniel Wilson's
efforts — the Society played a major role in various campaigns to
preserve the rapidly disappearing buildings of Edinburgh. Amongst
the first was the restoration of St Margaret's Chapel. Other campaigns were less successful, for example the attempt to save the
fifteenth century Trinity College Chapel, which was ultimately
demolished to make way for Waverley Station shunting yard. Yet
from this defeat came Lord Cockburn's 'Letter to the Lord Provost
on the best ways of spoiling the beauty of Edinburgh' and the
beginnings of the Edinburgh Civic movement.

The Antiquaries' campaign to save their Museum collection was
more immediately successful. Agreement in principle was reached in
1848: if the Society would put their house in order the government
would take over the collection.

Daniel Wilson set to work reorganising the Antiquaries' Museum.
It was not an easy task because it contained everything from the
Edinburgh guillotine, 'The Maiden', and Sir Walter Scott's chair, to
the most primitive stone implements. It is difficult to understand
how little was known in the mid-nineteenth century of the progression of human societies before the survival of written documents.

There were few guidelines beyond the philosophical speculations of such eighteenth century thinkers as Lord Kames, Adam Smith, Adam Ferguson and John Miller. The problem was even more acute when it came to physical remains, such as buildings and artefacts. Speculation about such things as stone circles and arrowheads was rife: a common response was to assign buildings such as brochs and stone circles indiscriminately to Druids, Romans or Danes, or even posit a supernatural origin for such objects as stone arrowheads — hence the common Scottish term for them, 'elf bolts'. There was not even a word to describe history before written documents, hence Daniel Wilson's invention of the English word, 'prehistoric'.

Wilson believed that archaeology was a science and that it should be organised in a scientific manner — within ordered groupings analogous to chemical elements or families of plants and animals. The system he chose for this new science came from Denmark. The Scottish Antiquaries had long maintained connections with Scandinavian archaeologists, who were the most advanced in Europe. In the early decades of the nineteenth century, a system of archaeological classification had been worked out in the Copenhagen Museum based on materials: stone, bronze and iron. Daniel Wilson was the first British archaeologist to use the now standard stone, bronze and iron age system in his reorganization of the Antiquaries' Museum. The great strength of the 'three-age system' was its flexibility: it could be applied everywhere — from Europe (which had passed through all three stages, and was even then passing on to 'the age of steel') to still-existing stone age societies elsewhere in the world.

Daniel Wilson was also one of the first archaeologists to use the exact sciences in the study of archaeological remains. For, example, George Wilson was enlisted to analyse a number of bronze artefacts found in Duddingston Loch in Edinburgh, and the differing rates of alloy he found illustrated neatly Daniel's belief that within these large general categories — stone, bronze and iron — there were huge variations: 'There are no true duplicates in the collection of the archaeologist. His researches are conducted in a boundless field, since their novelty is as inexhaustable as the phases of human thought.'

Daniel Wilson was also aware that new techniques such as photography could play their part in the development of a more exact science of archaeology. In 1848 his friend, D O Hill showed calotypes of 'Scottish topographical antiquities and portraits' at a meeting of the Antiquaries, perhaps the first use of photography in an archaeological context.

Daniel was grappling with many of the questions that had occupied the Englightenment social thinkers: how do social groups arise, how do human societies change, what constitutes civilization and how do we define it? For some of his practical answers to these fundamental questions, Wilson was influenced by the work of the English ethnologist, C J Prichard, whose *Researches into the Physical History of Mankind* had appeared in five volumes between 1836 and 1847, especially in his argument for a common origin for the human race (monogenesis), and his use of comparative anatomy, such as the study of cranial types, and studies of analogous societies.

By 1849 Wilson had finished his reorganisation and published a *Synopsis* of the Antiquaries' Museum collection, organised along the Danish lines with modifications to illustrate peculiar local features. Following Prichard, much of the Scottish material was displayed alongside analogous material from other societies, 'for the purpose of comparison'. The *Synopsis* became a sketch for Daniel Wilson's epoch-making *The Archaeology and Prehistoric Annals of Scotland* published in 1851; the starting point for modern Scottish archaeology and a landmark in the history of British archaeology as a whole.

Having laid the basis for modern Scottish archaeology, Daniel Wilson realized that there should also be a means of keeping the new subject up to date. He began a new archaeological journal, *Proceedings of the Society of Antiquaries of Scotland,* which first appeared in 1854 and continues to the present day as the major Scottish archaeological journal.

Prehistoric Annals received high praise when it was published and Wilson and his friends clearly hoped that it — and his other achievements — would lead to an academic or scholarly position in Britain. Instead in 1853 he was appointed to the newly-created chair of History and Literature at University College, Toronto. Within days of his arrival in Philadelphia *en route* for Canada, Daniel Wilson was caught up in some of the controversies that would mark his second career as Canada's first anthropologist. *Prehistoric Annals* had also been well received in North America, and Wilson found himself lionised by American scientific circles, but he was horrified by the theories of the 'scientific racists' of the United States, who argued for the separation of whites, blacks and Indians on the grounds that they were separate species which, if interbred, would produce inferior or even infertile offspring. Wilson's belief in monogenism and his studies of the differing Scottish prehistoric crania had convinced him that the modern population of his native country was the result of a fusion of different races over thousands of years.

In North America, he believed he could see this process of racial fusion taking place before his very eyes: the whole continent was a kind of anthropological laboratory where races met and mixed and where civilizations rose and fell. Unlike the scientific racists Wilson saw such change as a positive thing: in the *métis* of Canada, for example, he saw a new vigorous hybrid American race. Daniel Wilson became one of the most outspoken critics of scientific racism in North America in the years leading up to the American Civil War, and remained a champion of black and Indian rights throughout his life.

Within a few months of his arrival in Canada, he was immersed in the study of the Indian peoples of his new country, that was to lead to the publication of his second great work, a study of North American ethnology, *Prehistoric Man,* in 1862.

For both Daniel and George Wilson scholarship was not a remote or static thing; just as society progressed, so did science. Thus both archaeology and chemistry had not only a theoretical context but an equally important social one. Science also had a transcendent quality. When, in 1851, George Wilson went to the Great Exhibition in London and visited the Crystal Palace he saw it not only as a remarkable piece of engineering but also as a spiritual metaphor — the Palace's arc of glass and steel paralleling the arc of the skies: one the work of man, the other of God. Both Wilson brothers were deeply religious men who saw scientific truth as part of divine truth: indeed, Daniel Wilson's regard for 'truth' led him to accept Darwinian theory soon after the publication of *Origin of Species* in 1859, however much he disliked what he saw as Darwin's own personal lack of a spiritual sense.

George's ill-health, and the feeling that his life was to be a short one, added force not only to his sense of the moral qualities of science but also to his own personal character. John Stuart Blackie said of him: 'I never knew a man of more beautiful and loving nature. To be in his company for half-an-hour was like reading a chapter of St John.' The period between 1844 and 1854 was full of intense activity for George, astonishing in so frail a man, who was now also suffering from consumption of the lungs. In addition to his lectures and experimental work, George Wilson became increasingly interested in the history of science — his *Life of Cavendish* was published in 1851 to general praise. He was also deeply concerned with the practical application of science. His chemistry textbook, published by Robert Chambers in 1849, went through a number of editions until the 1870s. His tests on over 1,000 subjects led to a series of papers on the practical problems of colour-blindness in the new technological age; 'On Railways and ship signals in relation to colour blindness' (1853). But his greatest work was to be as first director of the Industrial Museum of Scotland (later the Royal Scottish Museum and now part of the Royal Museum of Scotland).

In 1851 the world had travelled to London to see the Great Exhibition. This gathering together of the fruits of the new technologies that had made Britain the workshop of the world led to a movement to set up museums of 'manufactures' throughout Britain. In 1854 Parliament voted £7,000 to purchase a site in Edinburgh for a 'Scottish Industrial Museum'. Not only was the new institution to display manufactures of all kinds, it was to be a centre for general popular education with a library and a regular lecture series.

There was little doubt that George Wilson was the best qualified person for the position of director of this new Museum. Because the University of Edinburgh was unwilling that the new Museum hold lectures that might compete with their own, a special Chair of Technology was created for the new director: George obtained his Edinburgh professorship at last. The post of Museum Director allowed George to give up the wearying round of lecture courses that so sapped his small strength and concentrate his energies on one thing: 'I am determined to let no day pass without doing something for my dear Museum.'

Like Daniel before him, the first problem he faced was one of definitions. His inaugural lecture in 1854 was entitled, 'What is Technology?' and by 1855 he was able to say 'Technology prospers and people are learning how to spell it . . . *Science in its application to the Useful Arts* is the meaning of the word.' George spent much of his time lecturing on behalf of his new Museum, constantly emphasising its usefulness not only in practical affairs but as an agent for developing personal character.

The next problem was how the Museum was to be organised. Unlike Daniel, George could not use materials as his basis. Instead function and purpose were the determining factors:

An Industrial Museum is intended to be a repository for all the objects of useful art, including the raw materials with which each article deals, the finished products into which it converts them, drawings and diagrams explanatory of the processes through which it puts these materials, models or examples of the machinery with which it prepares and fashions them, and the tools which specially belong to development and analogies, and the social

Nº 34

Cumbĕuk. *N. Name*

Little known to the Sealers.

Colour drawing by Neill of a fish with the Australian aborigine name of Cumbeuk, collected by Neill at King George's Sound. (By permission of the Trustees of the British Museum (Natural History))

Watercolour by Daniel
Wilson of Greyfriars
Churchyard. This may
have been painted from
the window of his
brother George's rooms
in Brown Square.
(Edinburgh University
Library)

Athapaskan hunting bag given to the Industrial Museum of Scotland by Robert Campbell of the Hudson's Bay Company, through the good offices of the Company's Overseas Governor, George Simpson. (NMS)

context of production and use.

Like Daniel, George believed that Britain was the most advanced nation on earth but he also believed that all men were equal in the sight of God and all invention sprang from a common human condition: 'Half of the Industrial Arts are the result of our being born without clothes; the other half of our being born without tools.' So, in addition to collecting everything from minerals, raw materials and the most sophisticated of modern inventions and industrial processes, he also collected examples of the work of what he called 'Savage technologists'. One of the first people he applied to for help was his brother who had spent the summer of 1855 on a trip to visit the Indian tribes of Lake Superior. In the following year George wrote in his weekly letter to Daniel: 'Is it at all possible to procure specimens of Red Indian work for the Museum?' Daniel contacted Sir George Simpson of the Hudson's Bay Company, who arranged for a number of his Company factors (many of whom were Scotsmen) to collect material from the Athabaskan-speaking Indians of north central Canada for the new Museum. Over the next few years cases were shipped from remote Company Forts to Edinburgh containing finished ('manufactured') articles, as well as items at various stages of completion and models of articles too large to send (such as canoes).

The Athabaskan Indian collection is remarkable for its complete documentation: schedules were drawn to be filled in by the collectors, including notes on the provenance of the articles, tribal origins and materials, and methods of manufacture. It is not hard to detect the hand of George and Daniel Wilson in this concern for

The crosier of St Fillan, returned to Scotland from Canada by Daniel Wilson, (NMS)

ordered documentation of the products of *all* human societies. Like Adam Smith, they saw human progress in terms of technological advance that met immediate human needs. Societies advanced at different rates and developed different answers to their requirements depending on local conditions, but overall human change was the same — a progression from rudeness to refinement.

Despite delays in voting money for the Museum building, by the time of George Wilson's death in November 1859 over 10,000 specimens had been collected. Edinburgh held a public funeral for George Wilson. Large crowds turned out to watch the funeral cortege, with its escort of civic dignitaries, pass on its way from the family home to the Old Calton burial ground, where George was buried beneath a Celtic cross.

When Daniel had gone to Canada, everyone had hoped that someday he would return to a position in Scotland. A few months before he died, George had written to Daniel:

> Oh, that they would put the antiquaries' museum under the same roof as mine and make you Professor of Archaeology and let us devise monograms and plan museums and lecture rooms etc as in the old schoolboy days.

It would take nearly 130 years before this dream would come true in the union of the National Museum of Antiquities of Scotland and the Royal Scottish Museum in 1985.

Daniel Wilson spent the second half of his life in Canada, becoming one of that country's most distinguished early scientists and educators. Despite his success, however, he remained an exile, with Scotland and his beloved Edinburgh always in his thoughts. When he had been writing *Prehistoric Annals* in the 1840s, he had first made enquiries into the whereabouts of the Quigrich, the medieval Crosier of St Fillan, which Robert the Bruce was supposed to have had in his tent on the eve of the battle of Bannockburn in 1314. He found that it had been taken to Canada by its hereditary keeper in 1818. At last, in 1877, he was able to purchase it for *his* Edinburgh museum. When he learned of its safe arrival in Scotland, he wrote: 'It is something to have accomplished this, if no more, for dear auld Scotland.'

Daniel Wilson became President of the University of Toronto in 1880 and was knighted for his services to Canadian education. When he died in 1892, Sir Daniel Wilson was buried beside his beloved wife in St James Cemetery in Toronto. Like his 'dear brother and best friend', he too lies under a Celtic cross, overlooking a Canadian Don Valley, and facing east towards home.

John Hope was Regius Keeper of Edinburgh's Botanic Garden from 1761 to 1786. At that time the Garden occupied the area where Haddington Place, Leith Walk now stands. The origins of the Botanic Garden, which was founded by Andrew Balfour and Robert Sibbald, originators also of the Edinburgh University Natural History Museum, lay in the need to cultivate plants for medical purposes. By the 19th century Scottish plant collectors were amongst the most adventurous and successful in the world.

SCOTTISH PLANTSMEN

Brinsley Burbidge

Ask any enthusiastic gardener to list some great Scottish gardens and it is unlikely that his total will exceed half a dozen, but ask him to name a few Scottish plantsmen, gardeners or plant collectors and the list will be much longer: Forrest, Fortune, Douglas, Cox, Menzies, Masson, Balfour, Sheriff and Forsyth quickly come to mind. All have been immortalised in the names of plants and most have achieved their fame outside Scotland.

The earliest well documented member of this band of great botanical explorers is Francis Masson (1741-1805), an Aberdonian, who was the first plant collector sent out from Kew. In October 1772 he arrived at the Cape of Good Hope. By the end of December he had organised the first shipments of plants back to Sir Joseph Banks, the director of Kew. Almost none of the extraordinarily rich Cape flora was then cultivated in Britain: the country was in the control of the Dutch East India Company and the few bulbs and living plants which had reached Britain had come by way of Holland.

After two preliminary excursions Masson teamed up with Carl Thunberg, the Swedish botanist and pupil of the great Carl Linnaeus. Thunberg spent some five years at the Cape, much of it collecting with Masson. They were a curious mixture of personalities, Masson the burly, dependable, slow gardener and Thunberg the small, egocentric, academic botanist. They had no language in common apart from a few words of botanical Latin and yet the partnership appeared to work. Their first journey together covered over 1,000 miles in the area between Cape Town and the Karoo. They travelled by ox wagon, with a vast supply of boxes and bags for collecting bulbs and seeds, and paper and presses for dry plant specimens. Masson's diary shows his enthusiasm for the areas through which they passed on their way to the arid lands of the great and little Karoo. 'The whole country affords a fine field for the botanist, being enamelled with the greatest number of flowers I ever saw of exquisite beauty and fragrance.' Masson collected over 100 Cape heaths, many gladioli, gazanias, romuleas, irises and more familiar Cape plants such as mesembryanthemums (of which he found 70) and the white arum lily, *Zantedeschia aethiopica*. In all Masson added over 400 new species to the Kew Collection.

It was Masson who solved the mystery of the origin of *Nerine sarniensis,* the Jersey lily. Despite its name (*sarniensis* means belonging to the Channel Islands), it was thought to come from Japan as it first arrived in Britain aboard a Japanese ship which was wrecked in the Channel Islands. Only when Masson discovered its true home on Table Mountain above Cape Town was its correct origin known. Presumably the Japanese ship had stopped at the Cape on its way to Britain.

After travels to Madeira, the Azores, the Canaries, the West Indies and again to South Africa, he embarked (in 1779) on his last voyage

David Douglas, intrepid plant collector in Canada, best remembered for the Douglas fir. (Royal Botanic Garden)

of exploration, this time to Canada. On the way the ship was twice attacked by pirates and finally sunk. Masson and some of the crew were picked up by a German ship which reached New York in December after some appalling bad weather. Little is known of his travels in Canada except that many beautiful plants including *Trillium grandiflorum* were returned to Kew. He died in Canada after the bad winter of 1804-5.

Another noted 18th century gardener was William Forsythe (1737-1804), a contemporary of Masson, also from Aberdeenshire. He worked mainly in England, becoming gardener to George III and helping to form what would eventually become the Royal Horticultural Society. The early 19th century saw the first plant collector to become a national hero. This was David Douglas (1799-1834), whose story shows how collectors of live plants achieve far greater acclaim than collectors of material for scientific study. Thomas Drummond (1790-1835), a contemporary and fellow Scot, collected in Canada at the same time as Douglas and the two even travelled together at times. Drummond's excellent herbarium material (dried plants for scientific examination) went almost unnoticed but Douglas returned to public acclaim and a round of engagements and dinner parties so exhausting that he longed to be in the field again.

Douglas was born at Scone, near Perth. He was a poor pupil but a great naturalist and countryman. Early in his life he worked in various gardens, firstly at Scone Palace itself, than at Valleyfield near Culross, Sir Robert Preston's garden, and then in the Glasgow Botanic Garden. His first collecting expedition was to North America. This visit resulted in little except for a few fruit trees from the east coast, but his extended second expedition which began after the long sea voyage round Cape Horn to the mouth of the Columbia river was an enormous success. Within days of his arrival in 1825 he found the flowering currant (*Ribes sangineum*), the beautiful bramble *(Rubus spectabilis)* and *Gaulthia shallon* which now grows so well in the wetter parts of Scotland that it is almost a major weed. Californian poppy *(Escholzia)*, Monkey musk *(Mimulus)* and poached-egg plant *(Limnanthes douglasii)* soon followed. Conifers were his forte and for these western North America is a perfect hunting ground. His most famous conifer is Douglas fir, *(Pseudotsuga menziesii)*, which commemorates not only Douglas's name but also that of another great Scottish collector, Archibald Menzies of Aberfeldy, the man who introduced the Monkey Puzzle. The original Douglas fir still stands in the grounds of Scone Palace.

Douglas had the usual explorer's disasters. On his way down the Fraser River his canoe was smashed to pieces in a series of rapids and all his botanical notes, collections and journals were lost. Douglas miraculously escaped after forty minutes spinning in a whirlpool. He visited the Hawaiian islands several times and it was there that he met his gruesome end, falling into a pit dug to trap cattle, which already held an enraged bull. Douglas was gored to death.

Just as the Royal Horticultural Society financed Douglas's expeditions to bring back plants for its garden and its members, so did the great nursery firm of Veitch finance many collectors to bring back plants of horticultural merit. John Veitch (1752-1839) was born at Jedburgh but went to England to work for a London nursery. Before he was 21 he began laying out the gardens of Sir Thomas Ackland at Killerton in Devon, and by 1808 he had set up his own nursery near Killerton. In 1832 the nursery moved to Exeter. Veitch's son James (1792-1863) gradually took control and was responsible in 1853 for the acquisition of a nursery in Chelsea which he called 'Royal Exotic Nurseries'. A third Veitch, also James (1815-69), ran the Chelsea side of the business and continued the Veitch line with his two sons John Gould and Harry James. The Veitch dynasty is complex and so is the extraordinarily talented group of plant collectors they employed. William Lobb travelled to California and South America and brought back the mis-named 'Scottish flame flower' from Chile. His brother, Thomas Lobb, one of the earliest orchid hunters, collected in the far east. The most famous of all 'Veitch's men' was E H Wilson (Chinese Wilson as he is better known). Wilson's original mission was to collect seed of the Dove Tree *(Davidia involucrata)*. In this he was successful, but he collected many other plants including one of the world's finest lilies, *Lilium regale*. The journey to collect this plant in a remote part of China put Wilson in the path of a rockfall which broke his leg. The long delay before it could be properly set resulted in a limp which remained with Wilson for the rest of his life.

Peter Barr exemplifies the specialist collector. He was born in Govan in 1826 and quickly left his first employment as a weaver to work for a firm of seedsmen. He gradually added to his expertise until in 1883 he founded his own firm, Barr and Son, which concentrated on the sale of bulbous plants, especially tulips and narcissi (daffodils). Pictures of *Narcissus cyclamineus* had worried him for many years as a drawing had featured in a 17th century herbal but had been pronounced by Dean Herbert, an 'expert', to be an 'absurdity which will never be found to exist'. Barr was not convinced and set out for Portugal to see if he could find it and to collect more bulbs for his nursery business. Not only did he find *Narcissus cyclamineus* but he collected an enormous quantity of many of the narcissi which are so familiar in our gardens today, such as *Narcissus triandrus* (Angels tears narcissus) and *Narcissus bulbocodium* (hoop-petticoat narcissus).

Barr returned to Portugal and Spain several times to ship home bulbs in quantities which would horrify any conservationist. At the age of 72 he went on a seven year world tour to publicise narcissi. He became excited by *Coleus* plants in Fiji and started the coleus craze when he returned to Britain. Ever one for trying new plants, he began growing *Primulas* at the age of 81 and claimed to have had over 1,000 species and varieties.

The most important area of the world from which plants hardy in the British Isles have been introduced is that extending from the central Himalayas eastward to the coast of China. The careers of two of Scotland's greatest sons, Robert Fortune and George Forrest, show dramatically the effect that the opening up of this region had on the plants we grow in British gardens. Robert Fortune (1812-80) from Blackadder in Berwickshire began his horticultural career at the Royal Botanic Garden, Edinburgh. From there he moved to the Horticultural Societies' Garden in Chiswick. As a result of the 1840 opium war and the Treaty of Nanking which followed, Britain was granted easier access to the interior of China as well as the port of Hong Kong. The Horticultural Society responded by sending the 31 year old Fortune to China in 1843 with tea plants high on the list of plants he was asked to collect. Despite the treaty, travel was still very dangerous. Fortune's response was to wear Chinese dress, grow a pigtail and shave the rest of his head so as to appear less conspicuous. His return to Britain with some 200 living plants including chrysanthemums, camellias, azaleas and other now common-place plants such as the wind-flower *(Anemone hupehensis)* and *Jasminium rudiflorum*, at that time making their debut outside China, was a triumph. His almost immediate appointment as curator of the Chelsea Physic Garden was rapidly followed by a return to China on behalf of the East India Company. From this journey came some 20 cases of tea plants as well as a small number of good garden plants including *Skimmia reevsiana*. He made two more visits to the Far East, including Japan where he spent some time collecting with John Veitch. Both their collections returned to Britain on the same ship. *Primula japonica* and *Lilium auratum,* both collected not in the wild but in Japanese nurseries, came back into cultivation as a result of this voyage.

Taking botanical exploration deep into China was a man generally acknowledged to be the greatest plant collector of all time, George Forrest (1873-1932). Forrest was born in Falkirk and educated at Kilmarnock Academy before he embarked on a series of adventures in Australia. He was 31 years old when he was sent from the Royal Botanic Garden, Edinburgh to China. Adventure began in his first year (1905) when he was staying at a small mission post just south of the China-Tibet border. The Tibetans, enraged by the Young-Husband expedition which they took to be an invasion of Tibet, launched a full scale attack from the north bent on slaughtering Chinese and European alike. Forrest's party of 17 together with the missionaries and about 60 Chinese escaped to the south but were rapidly overtaken. Only 14 escaped the ensuing massacre and Forrest was the only survivor of his own party. It took him over 20 days to find his way to safety by which time notification of his 'death' had already been sent to his family and friends in Edinburgh.

Forrest was not deterred and returned many times to China where he spent a total of 17 years. His collections were remarkable with over 40,000 separate gatherings including literally hundreds of new rhododendrons and primulas and one of the best of all gentians, *Gentiana sino-ornata*. He also collected some fine Himalayan blue poppies, many lilies and a great number of dwarf 'alpine' plants. It is

George Forrest, one of
the greatest plant
collectors of all time.
(Royal Botanic Garden)

for the genus Rhododendron that he will be most remembered.
Among the 309 of his plants which were described as species new to
science, 12 received the First Class Certificate of the Royal Horticultural Society for excellence for garden plants and no fewer than
48 received their award of merit.

There were many more Scots who made an impact on horticulture.
A few, such as John Hutton Balfour and Isaac Bayley Balfour (father
and son), both Regius Keepers of the Royal Botanic Garden, Edinburgh achieved success at home, but the great majority made their
names in exile. Perhaps this is not so remarkable when the small
number of plants (few really garden-worthy) found in Scotland are
considered, but that only explains why collectors and explorers left
their native land. Gardeners have less reason for leaving home as the
west of Scotland provides one of the world's best climates for growing many exotic plants, especially the conifers and rhododendrons.
Remarkable amongst 'those who stayed' was Osgood MacKenzie,
who at the end of the last century and the beginning of this made the
remarkable garden of Inverewe from what was nothing more than a
heather-clad peninsula in Wester Ross.

Perhaps the most plausible explanation for the tendency to
migrate south comes in a delightful statement by Stephen Switzer, the
horticultural writer, in 1718. 'There are several northern lads, which
whether they have served time in their art, or not, very few of us
know anything of; yet by the help of a little learning and a great deal
of impudence they invade these southern provinces; and the natural
benignity of this warmer climate has such a wonderful influence on
them, that one of them knows (or at least pretends to know) more in
one 12 month, than a laborious, honest south country man does in
seven years.'

The needs of medicine stimulated the collection and cultivation of plants. Scotland's medical reputation was worldwide. Edinburgh's first Infirmary was founded in 1729; the building above was opened in 1741. Infirmaries in Aberdeen, Dumfries and Glasgow followed later in the century. Scotland's leading role in medicine was paralleled by an increasing involvement in the sciences, for which Scottish universities became famous in the late 18th century. That involvement led in turn to the productive application of science to industrial development.

INDUSTRIAL ENTERPRISE AND THE SCOTTISH UNIVERSITIES IN THE EIGHTEENTH CENTURY

R G W Anderson

The question of how much the academic community in Great Britain contributed to the technical advances which are associated with the beginnings of the Industrial Revolution in the eighteenth century has been considered by various scholars, but a consensus view has yet to emerge. On the one hand, Peter Mathias takes the view that innovations were by and large not the result of the formal application of applied science and that formal scientific training was less important than determination and curiosity, 'quick wits, clever fingers, luck, capital, or employment and a backer to survive the period of experimenting.' On the other hand, A E Musson and Eric Robinson suggest that there was a relationship between the industrial revolution and the scientific revolution, that a 'knowledge of science was more widely diffused through industrial society than has hitherto been suggested.'

The five Scottish universities were of quite a distinct character from the English universities of Oxford and Cambridge. Science and medicine were being actively developed in Edinburgh, Glasgow and, to a lesser extent, Marischal College, Aberdeen. At Oxford and Cambridge, while science and medicine teaching was not as moribund as sometimes has been represented, these subjects were more peripheral (the main subjects being classics and theology) than in Scotland. Moreover, the English universities were closed to nonconformists, and it was among the intellectual dissenters that much industrial enterprise was to originate. By 1800, twelve chairs in mathematics, science and medicine had been founded at Edinburgh. Most were occupied by professors who were energetic and conscientious in their duties. In addition, a sub-culture of extra-mural teachers was developing; many of them would eventually be appointed to professorships. To the west, Glasgow University did not enjoy quite the same prestige. Nevertheless there were five chairs in the sciences and medicine by the end of the century, and two untenured lectureships, in chemistry and in materia medica.

The Scottish universities were involved in science teaching through both their arts courses and their medical schools. Natural philosophy (physics) was taught with the classics, logic and ethics for the degree of master of arts. Medicine involved the teaching of chemistry and botany. In addition there were chairs of mathematics and astronomy at both Edinburgh and Glasgow, and of natural history and agriculture at Edinburgh. Thus a scientific culture was well developed at University level and this was widely recognised. In particular, the Edinburgh medical school had a growing reputation, with students being attracted from distant parts of the globe such as America, the Caribbean and Russia. As it happened, relatively few students who attended the course intended to graduate in medicine at Edinburgh. Many came because of the renowned quality of the teaching; a significant proportion were already in employment and were established as scientists, doctors and industrialists.

The establishment of the Edinburgh medical school was one of a number of initiatives taken by the astute Edinburgh merchant George Drummond in an effort to revive national dignity in the period of low morale after the Darien disaster and the Act of Union. Drummond, who joined the Town Council as Treasurer in 1717 and was subsequently Lord Provost on six occasions, was aware of the success of the medical school at Leiden in Holland and was convinced that it could be replicated in Edinburgh, bringing the University international standing. In 1726 the first four professors of medicine (who had been carefully nurtured by Drummond) were appointed by the Town Council. Success was not long in coming and soon students were arriving from far afield.

The four, John Innes, Andrew Plummer, Andrew St Clair and John Rutherford were unsalaried; they were expected to use their position to generate income from student fees or from any other entrepreneurial venture. Almost immediately they went into partnership as a drug preparation and wholesaling business, and this was soon flourishing. The raw ingredients and apparatus were purchased from London in substantial quantities and pharmaceutical products were made up and distributed on a large scale: receivers for collecting the products of distillation were of four gallons capacity; and an order for 56 pounds of cinnamon was sent off. Five hundred copies of a catalogue were ordered from a printer in 1732. By 1734, the value of the laboratory and stock stood at over £960. This enterprise was closely associated with the rise of the medical school and it almost certainly provided a service unavailable on such a scale prior to its establishment. The professors were pursuing dual careers, as academics and industrialists. It is unlikely that such a business would have been set up at that time were it not for the university providing a focus for such men to be brought together.

Though undoubtedly successful as a businessman, Plummer taught a chemistry course which was not universally acclaimed. The main criticism was its narrow view of its subject — dealing as it did solely with pharmaceutical matters. One strong critic attended between 1734 and 1736: William Cullen, a ship's surgeon who was obtaining medical qualifications. In 1747, Cullen was appointed lecturer in chemistry at Glasgow, and recalling his Edinburgh experience, wrote 'the Pharmaceutical courses of Chemistry have not deserved the place they have hitherto held in our Schools, they are not fitted to lead us to a general knowledge of Chemistry, they are not suited to engage or facilitate an application to this Study.' Cullen's course of chemistry was innovative, and dealt extensively (but by no means exclusively) with how chemistry could be utilised. In his introductory lecture, he taught his students 'We propose to explain the general principles of the Arts depending on Chemistry and we shall often also shew the applications to particular Arts in such manner as the practices in the way of Trade and Business may be more easily understood and even improved.' (Here, the word 'Arts' means technical skills.) Cullen was particularly anxious to focus his pupils' attention on subjects of interest to Scottish industry. At another point in his course, he listed particular problems as:

'That of bleaching with less Sun or cheaper materials

That of Dying, particularly Linnen

That of Agriculture, the fixing its principles and preparing Manures

Most prominent Scottish chemist of the 18th century, Joseph Black's work was both innovative and of important practical application. From John Kay's *Original Portraits and Etchings.*

These then are a few instances of Chemical Inquiries which are particularly interesting to this Country and in which a discovery would certainly be attended with Profit.'

At about this time, Cullen struck up a friendship with Henry Home, Lord Kames, who was devoted to the improvement of his own estate and, indeed, Scottish agriculture as a whole. The correspondence between the two men is filled with comments on how this might be achieved and with other matters concerning industrial developments such as bleaching and salt manufacture.

Cullen tried to persuade his students to undertake experiments of their own in his laboratory. This offer was not taken up with alacrity, though one student leapt at the opportunity. He was Joseph Black, who was to become the most prominent Scottish chemist of the century. Black developed an interest in the chemical properties of alkalis, and when he transferred to Edinburgh in 1752 to complete his medical degree, his thesis was devoted to this subject. Alkalis were of great interest for two reasons: widespread debates were taking place concerning which alkalis were most effective in treating kidney stones (a particularly troublesome affliction at the time); and the need to find a cheaper substitute for wood ashes which had to be imported into Scotland for use in bleaching operations in the vitally important linen industry. Black's early research did not directly tackle either of these problems, although through the discovery of fixed air (carbon dioxide) it helped to characterise alkalis and established Black as a leading philosophical chemist.

In 1756 Cullen moved to Plummer's chair in Edinburgh and Black was appointed to Cullen's lectureship in Glasgow. Here Black taught in the tradition established by his predecessor. His research changed from alkalis to experiments on heat, and measurements were made of latent and specific heats. But like Cullen, Black was interested and personally involved in chemistry applied to industry. Ores containing silver and lead were analysed for Lord Erskine, enquiries from James Ferguson of Belfast on the bleaching of linen were dealt with, and the Carron Iron Works, established in 1759 as the first major iron-producing concern in Scotland, were visited by him.

During Black's time in Glasgow, he was introduced to the 'Mathematical Instrument Maker to the University', James Watt, by Robert Dick, professor of natural philosophy. Later Black wrote 'I soon had occasion to employ him [Watt] to make some things which I needed for my experiments, and found him to be a young man possessing most uncommon talents for mechanical knowledge and practice, with an originality, readiness, and copiousness of invention, which often surprised and delighted me in our frequent conversations together.' A strong friendship developed and Black went into a business partnership with him and Alexander Wilson (a typefounder who later became professor of astronomy). In 1763 Dick's successor, John Anderson, asked Watt to repair the University's model of a Newcomen engine. It was work on this which started Watt thinking about improvements to the steam engine which, ultimately, led to the partnership between him and Matthew Boulton, and the setting up of the Soho Manufactory at Birmingham to build the engines. Black and Watt were closely aware of each other's work, Black writing 'I was thoroughly acquainted with the progress of his inventions, and with the different objects that engaged his attention while I remained at Glasgow.' Black was also instrumental in arranging finance for Watt. In 1765 he introduced him to the entrepreneur John Roebuck, who in 1749 had been one of the partners to establish the sulphuric acid works at Prestonpans, and also the Carron Iron Works. Roebuck and Watt went into partnership themselves, and Watt's first design for an improved Newcomen engine was intended for Roebuck at Kinneil. In 1769, Black himself loaned Watt the money for his patent on the separate condenser.

James Watt was clearly bound up in the life of Glasgow University and was on equal terms with the professors. He was later anxious to stress that his relationship with Black was not one of teacher-pupil; he stated that he did not attend Black's lectures (though he said that he would have had a better understanding of the subject had he done so). Watt's main innovation, the separate condenser, which enormously increased the efficiency of the steam engine, did not originate in the theoretical application of Black's theory of latent heat. Nevertheless the relationship between them and others helped create an environment in which new ideas flourished. Moreover, it would be a mistake to conclude simplistically that Black was the pure scientist and Watt the clever artisan. Humphrey Davy wrote that 'those who consider James Watt only as a great practical mechanic, form a very erroneous idea of his character: He was equally distinguished as a natural philosopher and a chemist, and his inventions demonstrate his profound knowledge of those sciences, and that peculiar characteristic of genius, the union of them for practical application.' Black left Glasgow in 1766 to take up the chair of chemistry at Edinburgh, and the two men never again lived in close contact. But this separation was responsible for a life-long correspondence which was filled with scientific and technological intelligence. Indeed, they carried out a joint research project to find a means of manufacturing alkali.

One of the great challenges to scientists in eighteenth century Scotland was the improvement of the bleaching process for linen.

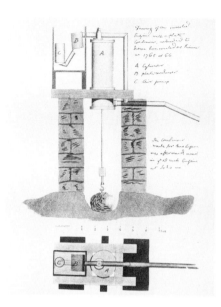

James Watt's design for an improved Newcomen engine, prepared for John Roebuck at Kinneil in 1765. (Edinburgh University Library)

Traditionally, soured milk had been used, though this was time-consuming and inefficient. Wood ashes, or potash, were very much more satisfactory for the purpose but this alkali was expensive, and had to be imported from England, Holland and France. Throughout the second half of the century, strenuous efforts were made by academics, industrialists and entrepreneurs, sometimes working together, to find a solution. Black suggested that if solutions of salt and lime (both cheap) were mixed together, then soda would be produced. Unfortunately the products of the reaction are also soluble. Watt and Roebuck attempted to solve the problem. They considered that if a paste were made of the starting materials together with sand, and if this were formed into bricks (and built as a wall), then soda would slowly crystallise at the surface. These experiments were being undertaken by early in 1766. Progress on the project was slow, and it was not until three years later that Black, Watt and Roebuck were discussing taking out a patent and bringing in a fourth partner, James Keir (who had studied at Edinburgh and was conducting similar experiments at Birmingham). Black was certainly performing laboratory-scale experiments, but with no great success. Though the scheme limped along for many years, it was never adopted on an industrial scale. Other efforts to improve bleaching were also being made. Francis Home, professor of materia medica at Edinburgh, proposed using dilute sulphuric acid, though this was considered potentially harmful to the cloth. The use of lime itself was widespread, effective, but also corrosive. Black himself had assessed this method in 1762/63 and declared 'I feel lime water will still be found a ticklish bleaching material.' The other approach was to search for native materials other than hardwood trees which could be used for making potash. Cullen experimented with conifers and ferns, Black with barilla and kelp (types of seaweed). But fern ash was too dirty and kelp yellowed the cloth. The ultimate solution, chlorine, was not to be found until the end of the century; again, it involved both university professors and industrialists closely working together.

There are two main claimants for the introduction of bleaching by

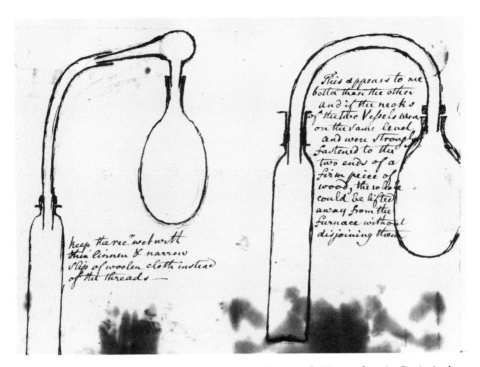

This appears to me better than the other and if the necks of the two Vessels were on the same level and were strongly fastened to the two ends of a firm piece of wood, the whole could be lifted away from the furnace without disjoining them

keep the rec.^r wet with thin linnen & narrow slips of woolen cloth instead of the threads —

Diagram of apparatus for linen bleaching, drawn by Joseph Black. (Edinburgh University Library)

chlorine gas into Britain: Boulton and Watt who, in Paris in late 1786, had visited a discoverer of chlorine and of its practical application to bleaching, Claude Louis Berthollet; and Patrick Copland, who learned of the process from the Swiss Nicolas Theodore de Saussure. Copland had been appointed in 1775 to the chair of natural philosophy at Marischal College, Aberdeen. In the spring of 1787 the Duke of Gordon asked Copland to accompany him on a European tour and at Geneva they met de Saussure (who had been the Duke's tutor), who told them of Berthollet's process. Back in Aberdeen, Copland informed Alexander and Patrick Milne of Gordon, Barron and Company, cotton manufacturers, of the process. This was a few months after Watt had persuaded his father-in-law, James McGrigor, a bleacher of Glasgow, to start experimenting with the technique. In spite of efforts to keep the increasingly successful method secret, knowledge of the use of chlorine spread in Scotland, notably to Charles Macintosh who was another of Black's pupils and who developed widespread interest in the chemical industry.

The use of chlorine in solution was an unpleasant process because of the poisonous and corrosive nature of the gas. The problem was largely solved by Macintosh and his partner Charles Tennant (yet another of Black's pupils) by absorbing chlorine in a slurry of lime, and later on to damp lime. In 1800 they established St Rollox chemical works in Glasgow to make the 'bleaching powder'. By the middle of the nineteenth century, the works were producing thousands of tons of it a year and it had become the standard agent.

There is a further economic factor to be considered in the development of Scotland's industry in the eighteenth century, and that was a form of state aid. After the Act of Union, annual sums of money were set aside by the government for this purpose and in 1727 the Board of Trustees for Manufacturers in Scotland was set up to administer the funds. Initially these were directed to the herring, woollen and (especially) the linen industries. The Board paid a

Rhododendron, one of
the many species
brought back from
China and Tibet by
George Forrest to the
Royal Botanic Garden,
Edinburgh. (Royal
Botanic Garden)

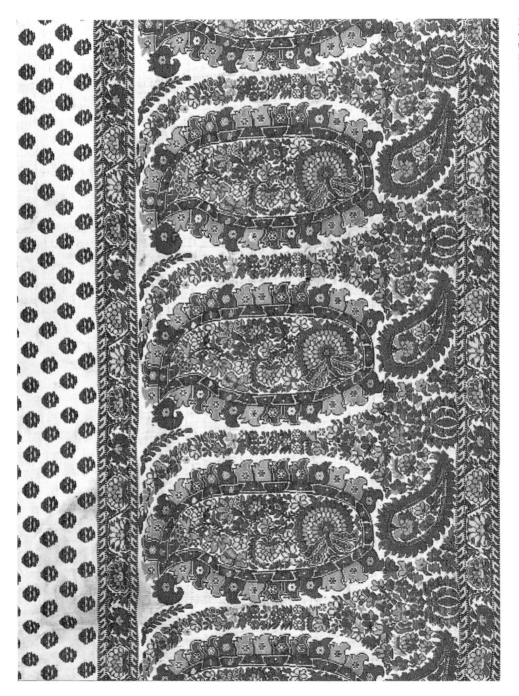

Border of an early 19th century shawl, showing the distinctive 'pine' motif. Woven in Edinburgh or Paisley. (NMS)

premium on flax and subsidised bleach fields, but it also awarded prizes for improvements, Home, Cullen and Black all receiving rewards for their contributions to bleaching processes. The Board also consulted professors when it needed advice. Correspondence between the Secretary to the Trustees, Robert Arbuthnot, and Joseph Black show that the latter was approached on matters as diverse as the design of an air furnace for smelting iron, improving methods of salt manufacture, production of alkalis, and vinegar works. Of course this is itself but a small range of subjects on which Black was consulted. It is quite clear that he became the obvious figure in Scotland to approach when advice was needed for industrial problems: The Earl of Dundonald called Black 'the best judge, perhaps in Europe' of industrial innovation.

In the later part of the eighteenth century a network had been set up of professors, industrialists, financiers and aristocrats who were involved in complementary ways in developing industry. There seems to have been little in the way of social barriers. Landowners sought out academics, aristocrats met with manufacturers, merchants and bankers, professors accepted invitations to dinner with students. This encouraged a free flow of information about new enterprises, and nothing seems to have been confidential for long. By means of correspondence, the network extended outside Scotland (especially to Birmingham) and, to some extent, to continental Europe. More directly, foreign students attended in significant numbers. The way in which the university professors were anxious to extend the education which they had to offer is noteworthy. Cullen, Black and Copland gave extra-mural lectures, as well as encouraging non-matriculated students to their normal courses. (One of Black's closest friends was the manager of a local glassworks who had attended his chemistry lectures.) On his death in 1796, John Anderson of Glasgow University left money in his will to 'Anderson's Institution', whose aim was 'to promote useful knowledge and improvements in Science and Philosophy applied to the various branches of trade and manufactures carried on in this populous City and neighbourhood'. The establishment of this institution was a most significant landmark in the development of technical education and, given the developing relationship between science and manufacturing industry of the previous half century, it is perhaps not surprising that it was due to the vision of a Scottish professor of natural philosophy.

Finally, an instructive illustration of the way in which the Scottish academic community was involved in developing industrialisation can be found in a biographical notice about William Irvine, a lecturer in materia medica and chemistry at Glasgow from 1769 to 1787. Dr Irvine was, apparently, always willing to assist and instruct manufacturers and had a direct personal concern with a sizeable glass manufactory. In fact at the time of his death negotiations had been completed with the Spanish Government which would have allowed Dr Irvine to reside in Spain in order to establish a glass manufactory until he became a Spanish citizen and could proceed to South America to superintend the Mines.

A public tribute was paid to Irvine's memory by the merchants and manufacturers of Glasgow who described 'the great advantage they had derived from the skill of Dr Irvine in the practical application of Chemistry to the Arts and Manufacturers of their City.' This was the spirit of Scottish scientific enterprise in the eighteenth century.

Dunfermline was a centre of linen production where handloom weaving, illustrated above, survived well into the 19th century. Improvements in bleaching techniques by men such as Joseph Black led to a revitalisation of the linen industry. Other textile centres, such as Paisley, moved into silk or cotton production. In the first half of the 19th century the Scottish textile industry thrived and exports were high.

PAISLEY: A TEXTILE TOWN

Jenni Calder

In 1779 the eighth Earl of Abercorn planned a new town for Paisley, on the right bank of the River Cart, with streets named after the town's trades and manufactures. Early that century Paisley had been described as '. . . a very pleasant and well built little town, plentifully provided with all sorts of grain, fruitts, coalls, peats, fishes, and what else is proper for the comfortable use of man'. Since then the town's manufacturing activity had grown, and with it its prosperity and its population.

Most of the activity was centred on textile production. In lowland Scotland the weaving of textiles from wool and flax had been a domestic industry for many centuries. It was not until the seventeenth century that Scottish woollen textiles began to be sold in Europe, and not until the eighteenth that there was a significant commercial basis for Scottish linen. It was then that Paisley became known for the manufacture of fine linen. The town's appearance on the mercantile map was partly due to the unsung heroes of Scotland's commercial rise after the Union of 1707, the packmen, who carried the products of the Paisley looms across the Border, where they found a ready market.

The Union stimulated textile production through much of Scotland, for it not only opened the door to England but gave Scotland access to markets abroad which had previously been the jealously guarded province of the English. Although unofficially Scottish merchants had been busy in these markets long before, trade in the lucrative colonies was now legitimate.

The fine quality of Paisley's products brought success in Europe. The numbers of weavers in Paisley increased, and they seem to have had an adventurous adaptability, which rescued the town more than once from periods of slump. By the end of the seventeenth century weaving already dominated the town's industry, and by 1730 an area of specialisation was being developed which gave scope for the Paisley weaver's individualism. This was the weaving of checked handkerchiefs in a light linen gauze, of which it was remarked that it gave weavers the opportunity to experiment with their own designs and to demonstrate their 'ingenuity and taste'.

With linen gauze production a proven success, in 1759, the manufacture of silk gauze was introduced. This has been attributed to Humphrey Fulton, who had come initially to Paisley to set up in the manufacture of linen and lawn. He moved into silk manufacture, with up to six hundred looms working for him. The quality of the silk produced was exceptional, the result, according to the *New Statistical Account,* of the 'inventive spirit, and patient application of the workmen' and the 'skill and taste of the masters'. It was a happy combination, for Paisley's silk gauze sold not only in the English and Irish capitals, but in Paris, and was said to excel the products of London's Spitalfield weavers, up till then kings of silk production. A

number of firms moved to Paisley from England, thus creating more employment for weavers, and by 1773 there were 876 looms producing silk, while 557 continued to weave linen.

More than most industries, textile production is vulnerable to changes in fashion. In the 1780s cotton, particularly fine muslins, began to challenge silk as a fashionable fabric. New inventions in spinning techniques were partly responsible. Hargreaves' spinning jenny and later Arkwright's spinning machine vastly accelerated the production of cotton yarn. Samuel Crompton's spinning mule of 1778 was another leap forward for cotton. In Scotland the growing cotton industry threatened the production of both silk and linen.

By 1789 silk weaving in Paisley had begun to decline. Cotton had come to town. It came first to a neighbouring parish, Neilston, which saw in 1780 the first modern cotton spinning mill in Scotland, converted from an old corn mill driven by the River Levern. Cotton spinning in Scotland grew rapidly, developed by a number of individuals who were quick to respond to the opportunities offered by the new technology. Notable amongst them was David Dale who, a weaver himself, was associated with initiating mills at New Lanark, Blantyre and Catrine as well as Spinningdale in Sutherland. In the wake of such pioneers came investment and expansion.

By the end of the eighteenth century spinning was mechanised but weaving was not, and this meant that there was more work than ever for weavers, with ample supplies of yarn for their looms. It also meant a decline in the status of the handloom weavers. Supplied by a machine they were part of a production line that brought fewer rewards and less satisfaction. Increasingly the Paisley weaver had to

Paisley at the time when the manufacture of shawls dominated the textile industry. (Renfrew District Council, Museums and Art Galleries Service)

produce what the manufacturer, and the market, demanded, with little scope for individuality. This decline, and ultimately degradation, of the handloom weaver was intensely felt in Paisley.

> In old times, every weaver, being his own master, came and went at his convenience; when he took a day's pleasure — fishing, curling, bowling, or berrying, as the case happened — he made up work for it before or after, as pleased him; the loom was his own property, and he was answerable to his employer only.

This writer, a Paisley weaver himself, was commenting on changes that he had experienced. The days of the independent and inventive weaver were coming to an end.

However, enterprise did not pass overnight from the hands of the weaver at his loom to the merchant and manufacturer. The striking feature of Paisley is the tenacity with which textile production survived, and the general acknowledgement of the skill and ingenuity of the weaver himself. In 1818 there were between six and seven thousand weavers in Paisley, out of a population of nearly 35,000. This was on the eve of Paisley's fame for the production of an item of costume that would prove an extraordinary success story.

In 1805 an Edinburgh manufacturer called James Paterson had some shawls woven in Paisley. Shawls had been produced in Edinburgh probably since the late 1770s when, inspired by the soft, light and warm shawls that were coming from north India, Edinburgh weavers (and also weavers in Norwich) began to specialise in shawls. By 1791 shawl weaving was well established, with records of one manufacturer, George Richmond of Sciennes, running thirteen looms weaving 'Indian' designs.

Edinburgh continued to weave shawls, but was quickly overtaken in production by Paisley. Shawls had come into fashion with the late eighteenth century vogue for lightweight fabrics and simple, classical lines. Indian shawls made from the hair of the Himalayan cashmere goat in designs that had originated in ancient Babylon had proved very appealing, and from the beginning there were efforts to imitate not only the designs but the weight and texture of the cashmere shawls. Silk, silk and cotton, and silk and wool mixtures were tried, and, although the latter provided a good combination of lightness and warmth, nothing was quite like real cashmere. Later, cashmere yarn was imported from France, where the goats were being successfully bred.

The early shawls were creamy in colour with a patterned border. Gradually the border grew, until by mid-century the entire shawl tended to be covered in a dense and often over-elaborate and unsubtly coloured pattern. The weaving of these patterns was an intricate business, and required a drawloom operated by a complex harness, which raised varying sequences of warp threads to allow the shuttle to pass through and create different colour combinations. The weaver needed the assistance of a drawboy, who was paid a proportion of the weaver's weekly earnings. Between 1814 and 1818 the first distinctive 'pine' designs, the motif that has ever since been labelled 'Paisley', were woven. In the 1830s the export of Paisley shawls topped the million mark, and by 1840 the Paisley textile industry was devoted almost exclusively to shawls.

The story was not one of unmitigated success. In those three or four decades there had been good times and bad times, and, although there was often plenty of work for the Paisley weaver, he was as subject as any other industrial operative to market and labour fluctuations. But in 1840 there were six thousand looms at work, of which the vast majority were engaged in harness weaving. The looms occupied the homes of the weavers, taking up most of their living space. Although their standard of living was relatively high, compared with that of other industrial workers, they toiled long and hard for their wages, often from six in the morning until ten or later at night. The Paisley weavers were traditionally an intellectually alert and investigative group of men, engaging in pursuits — reading, discussion, natural history — that encouraged self-improvement. There was also a spirit of real co-operation, with a ready exchange of ideas on how techniques and designs could be improved. But many inventions and ideas stemming from the weaver did not make the contribution they might have done because of the considerable expense involved in procuring patents. Many 'ingenious men of the operative classes', according to the *New Statistical Account,* were discouraged.

The Paisley shawl could not last for ever. In the early 1840s a slump in demand caused 67 of the 112 textile fims to fail. In a symbolic gesture of sympathetic support, Queen Victoria purchased several Paisley shawls, but this could not prevent their disappearance from the fashion scene. By 1870 they had gone. The plight of the weaver had been intensified by the introduction of the Jacquard loom, which mechanised the harness system and relegated the weaver to an even less important role in the sequence of events that produced the finished cloth. The Jacquard attachment was expensive and took up more space than was usually available in the weaver's cottage. Together with the advent of power weaving, it heralded the era of factory weaving. This meant the death not only of the craft of the handloom weaver, but of an entire culture.

Some aspects of weaving survived after 1870, with the old adaptability helping the industry to adjust to new products and new markets. There was still some demand for plaids and small shoulder shawls, and ponchos were made for export to South America. But it was not weaving that in the latter part of the century maintained Paisley as a textile town.

In 1721 a young woman called Christian Miller was left a widow. Living in Johnstone, close to Paisley, she supported herself by spinning linen yarn for thread. She was able to bleach it 'to perfection', and her white linen thread was so much admired that it was bought by lace makers in the southwest of England. Quick to build on this success Christian Miller acquired a thread-mill from Holland, and soon, with her mother and sister, had established a profitable thread-making business.

By 1744 thread-making was flourishing in Paisley, with 93 mills operating. By 1789 nearly five thousand people were employed in thread-making and Paisley was well known for a variety of high quality threads. The next chapter in the story of Paisley thread-making features two names which became virtually synonymous with sewing thread: Clark and Coats. They both set up in the Paisley area in the 1820s, and to both has been attributed the invention of cotton sewing thread. Whoever was the first, by the end of the century there were two Paisley firms pre-eminent in the production of sewing thread, Messrs J & P Coats and Messrs Clark and Co. Their success was partly the result of keenness and enterprise, helped considerably by the increasingly widespread use of the sewing machine and the growing needs of both factory and home dressmaking.

In 1889 the two firms co-operated to form a distributing centre called The Cotton Agency, later the Central Agency. Seven years later the firms amalgamated, by which time a large part of the world's thread industry was controlled from Paisley. They expanded into Europe, and as early as the 1860s had established works in the USA. It was a striking achievement.

For more than two centuries Paisley was associated with high quality products and with industrial and commercial initiative. The town's achievements were hard won. There were reversals and depressions, high emigration in the nineteenth century fuelled by frustration as well as lack of work, and often considerable suffering amongst those on whose labour the town's success depended. But the spirit of Paisley was remarkable, and it seems wholly appropriate that the town's enterprise should be remembered in the shawls that are now collector's items, in the pattern that has become a household name, and Coats thread which is used throughout the world. Visit Paisley itself, and the street names of the Earl of Abercorn's new town, Gauze, Silk, Inkle, Thread, provide forthright evidence of a productive past.

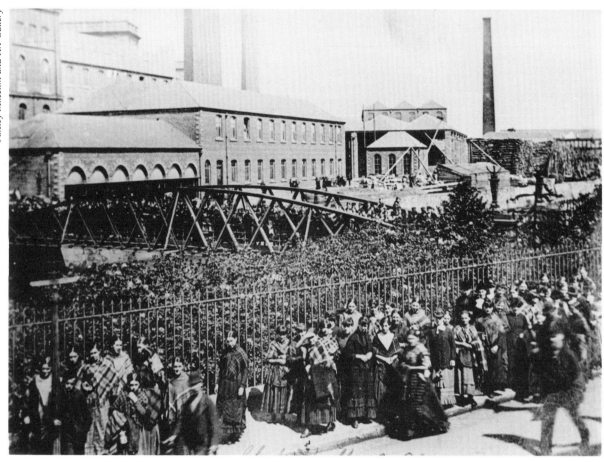

*Women workers at J & P Coats of Paisley in the 1890s, when
Coats was pre-eminent in the thread making industry. Factory
production had always employed large numbers of women,
although handloom weaving was dominated by men. The
needs of the factory and later of the office provided increased
employment opportunities for women, although there was
little scope for individuality or enterprise.
The second half of the 19th century saw a number of
adventurous and pioneering women entering the professions.
The impact of women in the medical and missionary fields,
areas where Scottish activity was very strong,
was particularly important.*

A BROAD, STRONG LIFE: DR JANE WATERSTON

Sheila M Brock

Jane Waterston was twenty-four years old when she arrived at Lovedale Institution, a missionary establishment of the Free Church of Scotland in South Africa's Cape Province. She was lively, energetic and filled with enthusiasm for her task of setting up a Girls' School to match that of the Boys' School which had been in existence since 1842. Jane owed her position as Head of this establishment primarily to Dr James Stewart who had persuaded the Foreign Mission Committee, and its formidable convener Dr Alexander Duff, that there was no need for the female Superintendent to be subordinate to a male teacher as had been recommended. James Stewart had achieved some standing in Free Church circles because he had accompanied David Livingstone on his Zambezi Expedition of 1862-3. It had been an unsatisfactory venture marred by disaster, death and, in Stewart's case, disillusion. Nevertheless Stewart was still determined to return to the African Continent and in 1864 was appointed to Lovedale. He delayed his departure for two years, while he gained a medical qualification from Glasgow University and married Mina, the youngest daughter of Alexander Stephen, the wealthy and successful shipbuilder. Jane Waterston and the Stewarts travelled together to South Africa in November 1866. It was the beginning of a close, and mutually supportive friendship. Jane lavished her warmth and sisterly care on Mina Stewart and the succession of 'bairnies' and constantly encouraged James Stewart in all his ventures, sharing many of his opinions and his aims. Her letters to him, carefully preserved (and published by the Van Riebecck Society) leave a vivid impression of mutual respect and affectionate friendship.

In 1869 Jane Waterston wrote to Stewart that 'a woman's life can never be the broad, strong thing a man's may become . . .'. This was written without rancour. It was an undergirding belief of the society in which she had grown up and, at that stage, Jane accepted it, although not entirely without question. Yet there were many women like Jane Waterston who aspired to, and achieved, 'broad, strong' lives. They did so, not with the approval and encouragement of society, but in an atmosphere of prejudice and hostility. For women to lay even limited claim to equality in the world of the nineteenth century required courage, especially to overcome the persistent feelings of uncertainty and guilt. In middle life Jane Waterston wrote:

> I have been thinking a good deal lately and have come to the conclusion it is useless for me to try and live as some friends would have me do and in the common acceptation enjoy life. It is useless. I can't, except in my own way. But a well done piece of work that has tried me to the utmost is simply glorious and I am going to live so . . .

In achieving such self-realisation, Jane Waterston enriched and

Jane Waterston, pioneer educator and doctor in South Africa.

enlightened many lives and made a distinctive contribution to the emancipation of women.

Jane Elizabeth Waterston was born in Inverness in January 1843. Her father, Charles Waterston, was manager of the Caledonian Bank and was able to provide modest comfort for his wife and seven children. Jane was educated privately and then at Inverness Royal Academy, but she spoke most disparagingly about her schooling, having discovered when she was faced with teaching 'raw, Kaffir girls' that her own education 'sadly lacked in the 3 R's', and she insisted that education for women meant 'doing away with the old, scrappy, tinselly, slovenly kind of stuff that used to be thought enough for a girl's schoolroom'. Nor did she receive much encouragement from her family. Her mother and three sisters all suffered, to some extent, from the Victorian complaint of 'hysteria', hypochondria nourished by boredom. At least one of her brothers went to Cambridge but none appears to have had Jane's strength of character or her competence. Impatience and irritation with this fecklessness, and particularly with the self-absorption and nervous behaviour of the women, were nevertheless a catalyst in Jane Waterston's commitment to education for women. She had learned that 'hysteria' had its roots in frustration.

And then comes the family Doctor, and friends whisper hysteria and a little tinkering is done with nervine tonics and change, while all the while, all that these exquisite cells want is to explode into purposeful activity, and so get rid of the pent-up energy which if not used threatens to turn into mental dynamite, and blow the unfortunate owner into a lunatic asylum, where in dreary vacuity the mind will at least find rest.

A significant influence on Jane Waterston, as on many women of her generation, was her Church affiliation and her personal religious beliefs. Schismatic movements in Scottish Churches, and attempts at re-union, theological debate and controversy, especially in the wake of Darwin's *Origin of Species,* formed an inescapable continuo which made itself heard in every aspect of life in Victorian Scotland. Charles Waterston had remained a member of the Established Church at the Disruption in 1843, but Jane, at some point, must have joined the Free Church of Scotland, attracted perhaps by its more evangelical flavour. Evangelicalism with its emphasis on sin and personal salvation, self-discipline and self-sacrifice had, by the mid-nineteenth century, significantly modified the rigid bleakness of Calvinist doctrine and had also rejected the nominal, rational beliefs of Deism in favour of commitment and conversion. This had an important paradoxical effect on the position of women. By their 'natural' qualities of virtue and self-restraint they were considered to be morally superior, untainted by the world in their domestic sphere of household and family and their autonomy in the education of young children. This attitude intensified the separateness of 'women's place' and their dependence. At the same time, the evangelical obligation to spread the Gospel message at home and abroad, resulted in an expansion of Church activities, Sunday Schools, distribution of Bibles or tracts, fund-raising and prayer-meetings. Participating in these, women gained self-confidence and experience in organisation, public-speaking and writing about a variety of concerns. Jane Waterston was a product of these paradoxical influences. Despite her personal disenchantment with domesticity, it was the virtues of 'home' and 'home-making' that she hoped to instill into the girls she taught in South Africa. Yet, her evangelical faith provided her with opportunities to voice her opinions at meetings, to expand and refine her opinions and, as it turned out, gave her the courage not to marry, not to conform to the traditional pattern of womanhood but to pursue an independent course.

By 1865, Jane was in touch with the Foreign Mission Committee of the Free Church and had offered her services. Although women were in the majority in Church congregations and, by the Veto Act of 1845, had the right to vote in elections of office-bearers, they could not themselves be elected and there was no thought of women being accorded positions of leadership. To some extent, an exception to this was in the Mission field where women were allowed to operate more independently, if only because certain social conventions were seen to be irrelevant. Not surprisingly, however, female missionaries were not paid on the same scale as men. Jane Waterston was appointed on £80 per annum and a small outfit allowance. James Stewart (admittedly older and more experienced) was paid £200 per annum and an additional £70 towards travel and outfit. His wife received financial assistance from her family, just as Jane Waterston's father gave her money to be placed in a bank in Cape Town, to ensure her return passage. In 1878 when she was older and less naive, Jane insisted on a more realistic salary for her journey to Central Africa and recalled the 'unpleasantness and inconvenience' associated with earlier arrangements and how in contributing to the Mission from her meagre salary she had 'got head over ears in debt'. Women missionaries were paid through the appropriate Ladies Committees of the Church. 'I have always received good treatment from the Glasgow Ladies Committee,' wrote Jane, 'and I am very much attached to the warm hearted and large hearted women on it but I simply detest the fashion in which the Edinburgh coterie does its work . . . Rawness, greenness and cheapness are what they want and very dear they have proved to be.'

Jane Waterston and the Stewarts arrived at Lovedale in January 1867. She spent the first year learning the Xhosa language and preparing the school which was opened in August 1868 with ten boarders. By 1872 an Infant School and a Work Department had been added and the numbers had trebled. The aim with which she began was 'not to turn out school girls but *women*' and not to do anything for the girls that they could not do for themselves. Nor did she hope to turn out 'pieces of black perfection . . . sprouting wings' as, characteristically, she observed that such 'incipient angels' were not evident in more advanced church circles. There was no point, however, in educating and civilising men only to have them marry ignorant, heathen girls and in all probability revert to the 'Red blanket'.

> The claim of Lovedale Girls' Institution was that
> there are now many furnished cottages presided over by women who have been taught the work which goes to make the physical comfort of a home and who have had these educational advantages which makes them companions and no longer merely slaves and beasts of burden.

In this way the Victorian conception of womanhood was transplanted to Africa but, although the expressed intention was to inculcate a sense of duty and service, Jane Waterston also maintained that rudimentary education was not enough — 'I do not think a native girl is educated at all, in the true sense of the word until she is taught

Classrooms of the girls' school at Lovedale Institution, Cape Province, South Africa.

to think a little for herself'. She was proud of the academic success of some of her pupils and several girls went to Scotland to continue their education including Letty Ncheni, Sana Mzimba, Tause Soga and Martha Kwatsha. In 1876 Martha Kwatsha was for a time a Sunday School-Teacher in Regent Square, 'a rather queer reversal of the ordinary line of things'.

The Girls' School had been built in the vicinity of the Boys' establishment at Lovedale. This caused some clicking of tongues, particularly amongst the Edinburgh Ladies, but Jane was relatively broad-minded and indignantly repudiated the insinuations of immoral conduct, at the same time enjoying a role as intermediary in romantic attachments between boys and girls. The important thing for her was that both should learn to be good workers and good scholars but above all Christians.

No distinction of race, colour or sect are recognised and no drones are allowed in this busy hive of men and women . . . no longer is it considered the distinguished work of a man that he can toast his toes in the sun while his mother or wife or daughter builds his house and tills his ground.

Dr Stewart appreciated Jane Waterston's qualities. She knew how to handle him and if both were sometimes difficult to get on with, both would have attributed this mainly to their intolerance with the lazy and incompetent. Not all her male colleagues found Jane so congenial and she, in turn, made no secret of her dislikes. For example, Dr Dalzell of the Gordon Mission in Natal had not, in Stewart's words 'sufficient esteem for the (female) sex as a whole to please Miss Waterston . . .'. When she expressed her strong views about 'women's rights and women's ability', Dalzell called her 'a philosopher in petticoats'. Although they eventually became more friendly, Jane considered him to be 'a coward, headstrong and coarse at the core'. By the African community at Lovedale Jane Waterston, was given the name of Noqakata, the Mother of Activity, or the one with the quick, springing step. It was a measure of the impact made by Jane's vigour and forthrightness in her relatively short-time at Lovedale that sixty years later the pupils at the Girls' School were still called Ama-Qakata after her.

The satisfaction experienced in this job was indisputable but Jane Waterston had further ambitions: to train as a doctor and to go to Central Africa where the missionary impact had so far been minimal. Stewart tried to dissuade her but his own medical training and his undisguised desire to return to Central Africa had almost certainly influenced Jane's decision. She wrote of her concern for those 'poor wretches of women up country' and of the obligation she, as a woman, felt for her 'black sisters'. In 1874 David Livingstone died at Ujiji, and, after his funeral in Westminster Abbey, it was James Stewart who proposed to the Foreign Mission Committee that they should establish the Livingstonia Mission on the shore of Lake Nyassa. Jane Waterston's intentions to go to this region were, as a result, focused on the new mission station.

She left Lovedale in 1873, spending three months at the Somerset Hospital in Cape Town learning to dress wounds and help in the operating room. Typically she chose to travel to Scotland via Zanzibar, Aden and the Red Sea. She was barely thirty but the years of responsibility and personal struggle had given her considerable self-confidence. Nevertheless she was nervous about the impact of her return to ordinary society.

> I am taking care to dress rather more carefully, than usual this trip . . . the present style seems to suit my bad figure. Even in Cape Town people remarked my dress and Mrs D Ross told me that I was not the hard, masculine woman she expected and that the black silk and soft white polonaise I had on when she first saw me was the very reverse of the dress she had expected. I am wearing dainty slippers and beautifully fitting kid gloves . . . and in fact am taking a wicked delight in disappointing everybody of the strong-minded woman they had expected to see.

Strong-mindedness in a woman was certainly required to overcome the obstacles in the way of receiving a medical education in 1874. The establishment of medicine as a profession and the rise in status of doctors in nineteenth century Britain was accompanied by protective legislation which excluded unqualified practitioners. Women, as midwives and herbalists particularly, had belonged to the latter category. The Medical Act of 1858 established the general medical register and registration was only possible through qualifying examinations from British institutions, but no University would award a woman a degree and hospitals were reluctant to permit clinical experience. Elizabeth Blackwell had qualified in America but that was no longer an option after 1858. Elizabeth Garrett (later Anderson) had obtained a license in 1865 through a loophole in the charter of the Society of Apothecaries (revised in 1868 to prevent such an occurrence), and Sophia Jex Blake had persuaded the University of Edinburgh to admit women to separate medical classes in 1869, only to have this decision revoked in 1874.

This ruling was made shortly before Jane Waterston hoped to enter medical classes at Edinburgh University.

As a result she went instead to London where Sophia Jex Blake had established the London School of Medicine for Women. The only hospital which would permit clinical practice was the new Hospital for Women, founded in 1872 by Elizabeth Garrett Anderson. By October 1874 Jane was 'working away at bones and other things'. She had an intense dislike of Jex Blake, passing the cruel comment that 'nature certainly made a mistake in making her a woman'. Nor did Jane think much of her abilities as a student for 'she made some very great blunders in an examination we had upon bones'. Two years later Jane Waterston commented that she herself was 'no favourite of Mrs Garrett Anderson's'.

> Mrs Anderson is very clever and does many a kind deed but . . . she blows me up whenever she has a chance for we are antagonistic natures, but I think she sees that I get on well with the poor women and girls that come about or are in the Hospital and I was one of those she wanted for a house surgeon.

Mrs Garrett Anderson was older and more sophisticated than Jane Waterston and her own struggles had turned her against the evangelical beliefs of her mother to the liberal doctrines of men like F D Maurice, who was a keen supporter of women's rights. 'I am too Scotch for her', wrote Jane and certainly she remained true to her evangelical beliefs, rejecting evolutionary theory and modern biblical scholarship. Still, she could not, and did not, avoid facing intellectual and personal issues.

> My life has been so different from that of most women I meet . . . that there seems to be a sort of gulf between me and them . . . I never yawn so much as when I get into a West End drawing room . . . which I do as seldom as possible. In Hospital or at hard study I feel comfortable or rather fresh and vigorous . . .

In April 1877, Jane Waterston went to Dublin's Rotunda Hospital, where she studied midwifery, gynaecology and ophthalmic surgery. The Kings and Queens College of Physicians in Dublin had agreed to examine women trained at Mrs Garrett Anderson's Hospital. Jane passed the first part of the examination in September and was licensed and on the medical register a year later in September 1878. She then returned to London to the Royal Free and the British Lying-In Hospitals to gain her licentiate in Midwifery. 'I can, if tired, pick up a baby any time and though I see much pain, I also see much rejoicing'. Jane Waterston, LKQCPI (Licentiate of the Kings and Queens College of Physicians, Ireland) and LM — only the official title, MD, eluded her as that was still closed to women.

Throughout this five year training period, Jane Waterston had never lost sight of her objective and in June 1879 she set sail for Central Africa and the Livingstonia Mission. This region was still remote and difficult. Several missionaries at Livingstonia had died from malaria, the slave trade continued and warring tribal factions unsettled the area. Travel was arduous but physical hardship did not trouble Jane, who remained free from fever and tackled the river trip and the march to Lake Nyassa with her usual energy. Nor did she object to travelling alone: 'I don't care a straw whether any woman goes with me or not, as long as there is the prospect of one being at Livingstonia for the sake of what other people think'. Yet, Jane Waterston's brief sojourn in Central Africa was for her an unmitigated disaster. She could not have arrived at a worse time. Missionaries in such isolation, frequently sheltering runaway slaves, had been faced with problems of administering justice and in some cases had imposed excessive punishments, leading once or twice to the death of the victim. Jane Waterston had heard rumours of this before she left Scotland and again en route to Livingstonia but the reality was worse than she imagined. To intensify her mood of apprehension, a Captain of the 82nd Prince of Wales Volunteers, whom she met in Durban, had recounted grisly tales of the Zulu War:

> . . . the cruel treatment of the Zulus was a cowardly deed, for the men who ordered it and did it would not have dared to do so to a white foe and in Europe. I guess there are some cowards in the mission Field too, who count on the "Dark Continent" hiding their deeds.

As Jane Waterston discovered, Livingstonia was not Lovedale and a single woman was undoubtedly in a vulnerable position in this atmosphere. Jane might have survived if the missionaries at Livingstonia had provided support but they were quite incapable of coping with an unconventional woman. Dr Robert Laws, in charge of the mission, did not appreciate her experience as a teacher nor her eagerness to practise as a doctor, and Jane was understandably infuriated by his insinuation that she had come to Livingstonia to find a husband. Within four months she had tendered her resignation. Jane Waterston has the distinction of being the first white woman doctor in Central Africa but, because of the circumstances, this fact has rarely been acknowledged.

In despair, Jane Waterston fled back to Lovedale. 'All the glory is gone from life and there is nothing left but just to plod away, earn one's bread and help others as much as one can'. Livingstonia had tried her faith and left her with a horror of religious humbug. The financial penalties of her premature resignation were considerable. The Foreign Mission Committee insisted that she refund her outfit and passage money, then struck her name off the list of missionaries. She was without position and without means.

For several years, Stewart's brother-in-law, John Stephen, had been planning to use his wealth to establish a hospital and medical school at Lovedale. This proposal had received no encouragement from the Foreign Mission Committee and it was to be decades before the ambition was realised. However in 1880, privately, John Stephen funded a small Medical Dispensary which provided Jane Waterston with an opportunity to practise medicine, the means to live and to repay the Committee. The Dispensary was an immediate success and she made a name for herself 'among the natives and also among the Europeans'. She was also something of a curiosity, and an object of comment in the local press.

> One of the celebrities of the Age, Dr Jane E Waterston, is at present at Lovedale, the lady who has scorned to walk in the beaten tracks of her sex and has *presumed* to prove that there are some of them as able to *fathom* the depths of science, penetrate and understand these mysterious fields of knowledge which the "Lords of Creation" have hitherto so jealously guarded as their own peculiar sphere. Perhaps it is as well that Miss Waterston is intending to labour in her profession among the heathen as prejudice against the sex might make her become regarded as an intruder by that grander, higher and nobler creation who have so much reverence for science that they do not like to see it become

Part of a model, completed in 1822 under the supervision of Robert Stevenson himself, of the Bell Rock lighthouse under construction. The temporary beacon or barrack is on the left, the base of the lighthouse on the right, and between them is part of the man-operated railway. (NMS)

Roseate or Ross's Gull.
The type specimen, shot
by James Clark Ross, is
in the collections of the
National Museums of
Scotland. (NMS)

common, by allowing ladies to become as clever as themselves if they can.

There was little future for Jane Waterston at Lovedale nevertheless. Despite her success with patients, she was working for a pittance and she flatly refused to take money which came even indirectly from the Committee. In 1878, the City of Glasgow Bank failure had had repercussions for her father's savings and the family's security. Jane had despaired for the 'four *helpless* women' who were 'fit for nothing but the poor house' and whose idea of economising was so inadequate it 'would make me laugh if it were not for the pain'. She, at least, had learned frugality the hard way, but she had also been trained for her profession instead of making future provision — 'better than putting it in a Bank certainly'. Now in spite of her profession, her prospects were bleak and financial independence was as elusive as ever. It was to achieve this independence, not to make a fortune, that Jane Waterston decided to go to Cape Town in 1883 and to enter into practice on her own account.

In 1884 Professor Henry Drummond from Glasgow visited her and reported to Stewart that she had given him 'a square talk of three hours and but for the fortunate advent of a patient I should certainly have had three more. She is a wonderful woman . . . she has a brass plate at her door "Waterston Physician".' In 1888 she returned to Edinburgh and passed examinations to become a licentiate of the Royal College of Surgeons. Later in June she became 'MD at last' with a degree from Brussels giving her 'great distinction'. Finally in July she obtained a Certificate in Psychological Medicine, an unofficial award which indicated an interest on her part in a comparatively young science.

Equipped now to her satisfaction she returned to Cape Town to set up permanent residence, partly to escape from her feckless family, partly because 'civilisation bores me and luxury does not suit me'. She had come to terms with her own guilt and sense of duty. Even so, when her father died in 1897 it was she who bore the brunt of the family's dependency. In June 1901 she sent money to Lovedale as a thank-offering for having finally cleared her father's name from debt, but she continued to send money home to her relatives.

At the age of forty-four, Jane Waterston was ready to take on the second stage of her life's work. She initiated the Ladies' Branch of the Free Dispensary to supply a public health service to women and children in the most squalid districts of Cape Town. This was later expanded to provide training for midwives and maternity nurses. For four decades, South Africa's first woman doctor maintained a personal interest in the Dispensary, lecturing to the students, attending cases. 'As a friend of the poor and needy, Dr Waterston soon became a legend in the City'. In the 1890s Jane Waterston was employed by the government to provide medical services for the leper and lunatic asylums on Robben Island and to deal with women convicts and prostitutes in the Lock Hospital. 'Nothing can make dealing with sin and vice easy work', she wrote, but her representations to the commission of inquiry into the operation of the controversial Contagious Diseases Act show considerable sympathy and common sense. Naturally, with these responsibilities, she was drawn into politics. Her reports on Robben Island were strongly critical of the government and privately she told them that 'if they did not mend their ways Truth and the Civilised World would turn in horror on them'. Jane maintained a keen interest in anything concerning 'Native'

Affairs, particularly with regard to Education and the Liquor Questions.

She regularly attended parliamentary sittings in the House and was personally acquainted, if not always in agreement, with Rhodes, Hofmeyer, Merriman and other notable Cape politicians. It was her boast that she entertained both government and opposition politicians to tea.

Before she went to Livingstonia, Jane Waterston had been advised never to marry if she wished to 'keep strong'. Possibly she had already made that decision as she attributed the family 'insanity' to the fact that her parents were first cousins, observing that 'mere human feelings, however sacred and strong must never be indulged in to the cursing of an unborn generation'. Yet, throughout her life, Jane formed intellectual and affectionate relationships with men, including Dr James Stewart and Professor Roderick Noble of the South African College, Editor of the Cape Monthly Magazine. In 1895, Edmund Garrett, a cousin of Elizabeth Garrett Anderson, became editor of the influential Cape Times, and he and Jane Waterston became close friends. This was a crucial period for South Africa, with political differences hardening in the aftermath of the Jameson Raid. Both Edmund Garrett and Jane Waterston were ardent imperialists, advocates of the Progressive Party and supporters of Cecil Rhodes and Lord Milner. Garrett consulted Jane on editorial policy and when he decided to stand for Victoria East (Lovedale's constituency) in 1898 it was largely due to her that he was returned.

War broke out in 1899 and Jane Waterston was involved from the outset in the organisation of relief for refugees. She praised the 'steady, sustained, businesslike work done by women with homes and families to look after'. In 1901 the strain was increased by an outbreak of plague in Cape Town, affecting the work of all doctors in the City. After the War, Emily Hobhouse's charge that the British had maltreated Boer women and children forced an official commission of enquiry. The Commission consisted of six women, including Jane Waterston, and was headed by Mrs Henry Fawcett, sister of Elizabeth Garrett Anderson.

In the remaining thirty years of her life, Jane Waterston confirmed her professional position, becoming a figure of standing — and some eccentricity — in Cape Town. She was President of the Cape of Good Hope (Western) Branch of the British Medical Association in 1905-06. In 1925 the Royal College of Physicians of Ireland elected her to a fellowship, only the second woman to receive this honour. The University of Cape Town bestowed an LLD in 1929, 'paying homage to the womanhood of South Africa'. She was probably the oldest woman practitioner in the British Empire and was certainly the doyenne of the profession in South Africa.

In 1888 Jane Waterston had delivered a paper on the Higher Education of Women. She compared conditions in 1877 when she had tried to attend a public meeting in King William's Town and was not permitted to enter without a chaperon. At that time she would not have been invited to give an address; even written articles had to appear under a nom de plume. She described the struggle she and others had had to gain a medical qualification and the risks run by those professional men who had helped them. Now 'the tide has turned for women at last'. Women wanted to work and to be paid for that work, even if they preferred some of the attentions and gallantries of the past. 'We will leave you the jellies and sweets, gentlemen, if you will share with us the beefsteaks'.

When Jane Waterston died in 1932, a Cape Times leader claimed that she had become a missionary from a 'plain Scottish sense of duty, informed by a deeply religious mind'.

'Her Scottish wit found ready expression, and her candour and fearlessness in the face of anything that she regarded as humbug could be as disconcerting as her gentleness of thought and action in the sickroom was beautiful.'

Throughout her long life Jane Waterston had fought for improved education for women and for the prestige of the medical and nursing professions. She had moreover advocated these improvements for both black and white in the volatile atmosphere of South Africa. When, in 1869, she wrote to Stewart that 'a woman's life can never be the broad, strong thing a man's may become', she added, 'but still, you might allow her to do what she can in the way of living. I like to live. I don't like to exist. JEW'.

For the vast majority of Scottish women the contribution to achievement was through a supportive role. The Scottish fishwife, however, was an independent and enduring figure, often tramping twenty or thirty miles with a heavy basket of fish on her back. Her seeking out of a market for the fish caught by the menfolk was a counterpart to the dangers they faced at sea.

Scottish fisheries were expanding in the 19th century, and this brought increased traffic in Scottish coastal waters, and improvements in harbour facilities and in measures to make navigation safer. The Stevenson family were at the centre of this activity.

ENGINEERS OF ENTERPRISE: THE STEVENSON FAMILY

Christine Thompson

In the late eighteenth century Scotland was a developing country. As her industries expanded so did her trade, both nationally and internationally. As a result, the surrounding seas, feared as some of the most dangerous in Europe, were increasingly frequented by ships. A wise skipper would avoid sailing at night, when the coastline was plunged into darkness relieved only by the flicker of a few coal-fire beacons lit here and there; but sometimes wind and weather gave him no choice in the matter and shipwreck was all too often the consequence.

In order to make marine navigation safer, Parliament passed an Act in 1786 authorising four new Scottish lighthouses to be built. The Act established a board of trustees or commissioners to supervise the erection of the lighthouses and they in turn appointed Thomas Smith, a lampmaker of Edinburgh, to be their engineer. Under his direction, the lighthouses were quickly built and equipped with oil lamps and reflectors which gave such a brilliant light that the Trustees were asked for more lighthouses. In order to cope with the increasing amount of work, Smith took on an assistant. This was Robert Stevenson, who later became successively Smith's step-son, apprentice, son-in-law and business partner. He also turned out to be the first in a long family line of exceptionally talented engineers.

Whilst working with Smith, Stevenson acquired the education and practical experience for what he intended to be his profession — civil engineering. From 1797, although Thomas was still the Commissioners' engineer, Robert took on most of his stepfather's lighthouse work while Thomas concentrated on the lamp-making side of the business. In the winter of 1807/8, the two men dissolved their partnership and Robert became sole Engineer to the Commissioners of the Northern Lighthouses. From then until his retirement in 1843 he was responsible for the building of eighteen lighthouses, the most celebrated of which is the one on the Bell Rock.

The Bell or Inchcape Rock lies off the east coast of Scotland, about 18 km (11 miles) from Arbroath, in the approaches to the Firths of Forth and Tay. By the end of the eighteenth century it was causing so many shipwrecks that public outcry demanded that it be marked with a light; and so Robert Stevenson decided to examine the problem.

After inspecting the site and studying what little information there was on building on isolated rocks at sea, he recommended a stone tower like the one John Smeaton had built on the Eddystone Rocks off the south coast of England. That very successful structure had been given a tree-trunk shape, circular in cross-section with a wide base and gently curved sides tapering towards a narrow top. In each course or layer of the tower, each stone was immovably dovetailed with its neighbours, while the courses themselves were prevented from sliding over each other by small cubes of stone inserted between them. To build like that on the Bell Rock would be expensive, but after considering several alternative designs the Commissioners chose Stevenson's, and construction began in 1807.

Despite having Smeaton's example to follow, Stevenson found he was faced at the Bell Rock with special problems that needed original solutions. The rock was uncovered only at low tide, severely restricting the time that could be spent working on it. So berths for the workmen were provided in ships moored nearby so that as soon as the tide fell, they could row the short distance to the rock and begin work. A temporary wooden beacon was erected where the blacksmith's forge could be kept clear of the waves. This structure was also intended as a refuge and, as work progressed, it was even made warm and dry enough to eat and sleep in.

Another problem was that of landing the specially-shaped stones on the rock without damaging or losing them. Stevenson's solution was to ship them from the workyard at Arbroath to the vicinity of the rock and transfer them to flat-bottomed boats which were then towed to the rock and along a gully to the landing-place. There each stone was hoisted onto a trolley standing on an iron railway. A man would then haul the trolley along the railway to the base of the growing tower. Here, two new kinds of crane, specially designed for the purpose by Stevenson, placed each stone exactly in its final resting place.

The Bell Rock lighthouse, completed in 1811, is now the oldest rock tower still in use around the British Isles. Its durability is testimony to Robert Stevenson's skill as a lighthouse engineer working under extraordinarily difficult physical conditions. However in accordance with his early determination to be a civil engineer, he did not confine himself to lighthouse-building. Just after finishing work on the Bell Rock, he set up a consultancy in Edinburgh and was soon kept very busy with requests to work or report on projects concerning harbours, rivers, roads, bridges, railways, canals, ferries and public buildings. He designed London Road and Regent Road, the roads into the eastern end of Edinburgh. He built bridges over the river Forth at Stirling, the Nith at Annan and the North Esk at Marykirk. In the course of his river-work he discovered that near the mouth of a river salt water flows upstream beneath the outflowing fresh water and he invented the hydrophore for collecting specimens of water from different depths. His investigation into the destruction of wood by a species of crustacean led to the widespread use of greenheart timber from South America for structures at sea.

He also wrote about his work. His account of the building of the Bell Rock lighthouse is well known. He made many contributions on engineering to the *Edinburgh Encyclopaedia* and the *Encyclopaedia Britannica*, and he wrote articles for some of the scientific societies to which he belonged.

Meanwhile his lighthouse work continued. This involved not only building lighthouses but also ensuring that they operated efficiently. Once a year he went on a voyage of inspection around the lighthouses; sometimes he took his children, hoping that they would follow in his professional footsteps. This hope was fulfilled, for three of his sons, Alan, David and Thomas, became civil engineers. Each was trained in his father's office and eventually taken on as a partner in the family consultancy. All three worked as engineers for the Northern Lighthouse Board, inheriting a lighthouse service which was largely the creation of their father and his step-father, Thomas

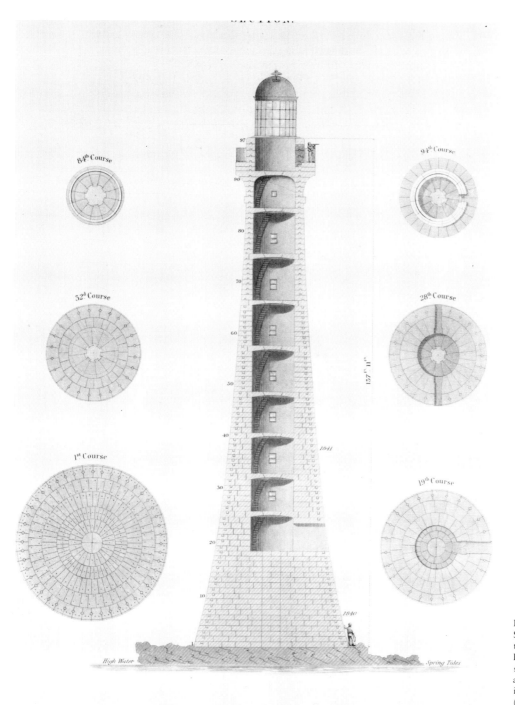

Plate VIII of Alan Stevenson's 'Account of the Skerryvore Lighthouse' (1848), showing the arrangements of stones in various courses. (NMS)

Smith. But they were not slavish followers of their father's example for they inherited a mixture of his personal qualities as well, including an aptitude for practical matters allied with inventiveness, a thirst for knowledge and a readiness to tackle the most severe of engineering problems. These characteristics led them to achievements which brought them reputations quite distinct from their father's.

Alan was perhaps the most versatile of all the Stevensons. His best-known engineering work was that connected with lighthouses. Early in his career, he became the Northern Lighthouse Board's expert on the latest in lighthouse optics: the Fresnel lens. This was a large specially-shaped glass lens which, when placed in front of a lamp, gave a more intense parallel beam than the old arrangement of a curved mirror placed behind the lamp. Alan was closely involved in the conversion of Scottish lighthouses to the new optical system, introducing several improvements of his own devising.

Just as his father was renowned for his lighthouse on the Bell Rock, Alan Stevenson was justly famed as the builder of Skerryvore lighthouse. Skerryvore is the largest rock in a cluster of islets and submerged ridges lying about 19 km (12 miles) south-west of the Hebridean island of Tiree. It presented a terrible danger to ships sailing through the North Channel between Scotland and Ireland and so had to be lit. The task of building there was quite formidable. It was lashed by frequent gales and had been polished to such smoothness by the Atlantic rollers that landing there was described as 'like climbing up the side of a bottle'. Nevertheless Alan and his workforce completed the job in six years, adopting the Bell Rock strategy of living in a temporary barrack on the rock and having the stones shipped out from a workyard on shore. To this scheme, Alan added his own touches, particularly in the design of the tower. He decided boldly to dispense with elaborate dovetailing in the lower parts, rightly calculating that the weight of masonry above would keep individual stones in place. In selecting the form of curve for the sides of the tower, he showed excellent architectural judgement. The result was an edifice of such stature and elegance that his nephew, Robert Louis Stevenson, later called it 'the noblest of all extant deep sea lights'.

In 1843, as Skerryvore was nearing completion, Alan succeeded his father as Engineer to the Northern Lighthouse Board, only to retire ten years later through ill-health. His place was taken by David, who had already earned a reputation as an authority on docks, harbours and river improvement schemes. He soon resigned the post, reluctant to take on the increasing amount of management and paperwork it involved, and instead went into partnership with his younger brother Thomas. Together they would work simply as engineers who would design and supervise the building of lighthouses for the Board but also have time to serve the Convention of Scottish Burghs and the Fishery Board and in general keep the family consultancy going.

The partnership of Messrs D & T Stevenson, as they were known, was long and successful. David seems to have been the better engineer while Thomas displayed an enquiring and inventive nature. He invented the wave dynamometer for measuring the pressure exerted by waves; and today the Stevenson screen — a white louvred cupboard — is still used at weather stations for housing meteorological instruments. Perhaps Thomas's most noteworthy achievement was the continuation of Alan's work on lighthouse illumination and the development of what he christened holophotes: optical systems which concentrated virtually all the light from a lamp into the required beam. By 1883, four years before his death, he had written 44 papers for scientific journals. This ability to write found full fruition in his son, Robert Louis, who spent some time working in the family office before devoting his life to literature.

David and Thomas built 29 lighthouses for the Northern Light-

Barns Ness lighthouse, near Dunbar, East Lothian, completed in 1901 under David A Stevenson as part of a move by the Commissioners to fill in the 'dark blanks' on the Scottish coasts. (Christine Thompson)

house Board, of which the most notable is that on Dubh Artach, an outlying tooth of the Torran reef off the Ross of Mull. They did not confine their labours to Scotland however; from the 1860s, in response to requests from foreign governments, they designed lighthouses, and trained the appropriate supervisors, for India, Japan, Newfoundland, China and New Zealand. For Japanese lighthouses, David invented the 'aseismatic joint' which, in the event of an earthquake, enabled the delicate lighting apparatus to stay still while the rest of the lighthouse shuddered.

The Stevenson tradition of engineering was continued into the next generation by two of David's offspring, David Alan and Charles, who eventually joined the family business. Like their father and uncle, Messrs D & C Stevenson were good partners even though they had rather different characters. David Alan was particularly interested in lighthouses and took the salaried post of Engineer to the Northern Lighthouse Board — the last Stevenson to do so. Charles concentrated on other engineering projects, such as bridge repairs, harbour surveys, river work and a variety of inventions.

Amongst the important lights erected during David Alan's 'reign' was that off Rattray Head, north of Peterhead, where a new departure in rock lighthouse design was introduced by Charles. The foghorn and its machinery were installed in the lighthouse, in a huge drum-like base, rather than on the nearby shore.

Another of Charles's schemes was the development of better communications with lighthouses. To this end, in the 1880s and 90s, he experimented with telephones and then, because of problems with submarine cables, with wireless communications. He was thus one of several people working on wireless just before Marconi took it out of the experimental field. A development of this work was Charles's radio-controlled mechanism for remote control of lights and fog signals. With help from his son, D (David) Alan, he also developed an electro-magnetic 'Leader Cable' for guiding ships through a channel. In 1929, D Alan and his elderly father unveiled their 'Talking Beacon', at Little Cumbrae lighthouse in the Firth of Clyde. This was a combination of a radio signal with a fog signal which enabled a fog bound ship to ascertain her distance from the lighthouse, in the same way that we count the seconds between a lightning flash and a thunderclap to see how far away the storm is.

With D Alan Stevenson, we come to the last Stevenson to become an engineer. Like his predecessors, he joined the family firm and experienced a wide variety of civil engineering work. This included being Lighthouse Engineer to the Government of India for a while, besides working for the Northern Lighthouse Board and a separate local authority, the Clyde Lighthouse Trustees. In connection with the latter, he deepened the Clyde channel in order to let the newly-built 'Queen Mary' leave Glasgow. In his final decades, having retired from engineering, he applied the Stevenson abilities for research and self-expression to the task of writing his highly-regarded book, *The World's Lighthouses before 1820*. He was still engaged in a family history when he died in 1971.

In the readiness with which they tackled difficult and dangerous work for the common good, in the way that they showed ingenuity and originality in solving problems, and in the way that they initiated and sustained a successful business concern through four generations, the Stevensons were striking examples of Scottish enterprise.

The Greenland whaling was an important factor in the increase in east coast shipping in the 19th century. By the end of the century Antarctic whaling was developing. Here the Balaena *of Dundee is caught in pack ice, c. 1910. The whalers contributed to the growth of knowledge of the polar regions, and in turn grew more adventurous as new areas were opened up by expeditions of exploration. Scots played a prominent part in expeditions to both the Arctic and Antarctic.*

Dundee Museum

PERILOUS ENTERPRISES: SCOTTISH EXPLORERS IN THE ARCTIC

Jenni Calder

'I was led, at an early period of life, by commercial views, to the country North-West of Lake Superior, in North America, and being endowed by Nature with an inquisitive mind and enterprising spirit; possessing also a constitution and frame of body equal to the most arduous undertakings, and being familiar with toilsome exertions in the prosecution of mercantile pursuits, I not only contemplated the practicability of penetrating across the continent of America, but was confident in the qualifications, as I was animated by the desire, to undertake the perilous enterprise. These are the words of Sir Alexander Mackenzie, from the preface to his account of the journey to the Arctic Ocean down the river that would be named after him. The combination of commercial acuity and readiness for adventure was characteristic of the spirit that opened up the northern American continent. Mackenzie was a man of intrepid confidence. He also had a certain ruthlessness, driving his men as hard as he drove himself in the encounter with the dangers of rapids and savage weather, and the ever-present threat of starvation and exhaustion.

In early June 1789, Alexander Mackenzie left Fort Chipewyan on the western shore of Lake Athabasca on a journey by canoe and on foot that would cover a distance of about 4830 km (3000 miles). Fort Chipewyan was the recently constructed headquarters of the North West Company's fur-trading activities in the Athabasca Department. In 1783 the Treaty of Paris, which marked the end of the American War of Independence, excluded British fur traders from the newly established United States of America, south of the Great Lakes. The North West Company, and the older Hudson's Bay Company, turned their attention to the northwest. The territory was largely unknown, but anticipation of prolific quantities of furs, particularly of the beaver that was so much in demand, encouraged this expansion.

Amongst the employees of both companies were many Scots; indeed, both companies had been largely initiated and managed by Scots. The 1770s had seen dramatic growth in the fur trade, pioneered by men like James Finlay, probably the first British trader to reach the Saskatchewan Valley from Montreal, the commercial centre of the trade. Alexander Mackenzie's connection with the trade began in 1779, when at the age of fifteen he joined the Montreal counting house of John Gregory, Finlay's partner. Alexander, born in Stornoway, had come to North America with his father Kenneth Mackenzie in 1774. It was a time of decline in the Western Isles, with poor harvests and high prices and rents encouraging an exodus across the Atlantic. Kenneth Mackenzie joined his brother in New York, who was already in business there. Then war broke out between Britain and the rebellious American colonies, and the two brothers became Loyalist officers.

Alexander's father died in May 1780, while stationed on Lake Ontario. In the meantime Alexander had been sent to Montreal. After five years at the commercial end of the fur trade he was eager to venture into the wilderness that was yielding such riches. Very quickly Mackenzie found himself playing a leading role in a new company, the North West Company, which had grown out of the increasing co-operation between traders anxious to exploit new territories. Leading figures in its creation were two Scots, Norman McLeod, who had taken over from James Finlay when he retired, and Simon McTavish, a man of ambition and perspicacity who made a great impression on another Scot with visions of development, Lord Selkirk.

Many of the Scots with both the North West Company and the Hudson's Bay Company, operating from the west shore of Hudson Bay, came from the Hebrides and Orkney, tempted by the prospect of independence and financial reward, and often leaving behind them a life of minimal subsistence and little promise of improvement. Scots were prominent amongst both traders and factors, those who made contact with the Indians who supplied the furs, and those who manned the forts and factories that acted as gathering points for supplies as well as the furs themselves.

Scots seemed undismayed by the rigours of the wilderness. Certainly Mackenzie tackled his journey to the Arctic with a degree of calmness. He was twenty-five years old, and already respected as a man of fortitude and leadership. The expedition which took him deep within the Arctic Circle was undertaken partly on his own initiative, although he was backed by the Company which stood to gain considerably from the exploration of new territory. Their main concern was the opening up of a route through to the Pacific Coast. Although Mackenzie's first expedition did not achieve this, it added greatly to knowledge of the northern reaches of the American continent — and in 1793 he successfully crossed the Rockies to the Pacific Ocean.

North of Fort Chipewyan lies the Great Slave Lake, and out of that huge and confusing expanse of water flows the river that took Mackenzie and his party of five men northwards to the Beaufort Sea. They reached the coast in the middle of July, but fog, rain and a 'hard north wind' made conditions difficult and visibility poor. Food was a problem, with game scarce and fishing disappointing. There was nothing to eat but mouldy pemmican, a form of dried and pounded meat. The return journey, against the current, was even more demanding, and often they could make no headway unless they towed their canoes. A day's travelling might begin at 3 am and continue for eighteen hours, with food supplies depending on what could be hunted or fished, or on co-operative Indians.

Mackenzie's journal does not dwell on the difficulties: in fact he records them rather cryptically. As he said himself at the end of the account of his second expedition, 'Their toils and their dangers, their solicitudes and sufferings, have not been exaggerated in my description. On the contrary, in many instances, language has failed me in the attempt to describe them'. A dour personality, perhaps, but determined, and with a courage and conviction that were not undermined by the vast and dangerous distances he covered.

Mackenzie's explorations brought within the bounds of European understanding two huge areas of what would become Canada. He discovered two great rivers, the Mackenzie and the Fraser, named for

Simon Fraser, another explorer of Scottish origin, and he was the first white man to cross North America. He reached the shore of the Arctic Ocean which had for two centuries inspired dreams of a short route to the riches of the East. Early in the nineteenth century the Arctic again became a centre of attention. The ice-bound straits and inlets were probed and charted as painful efforts were made to find the Northwest Passage.

If Scots were encouraged to cross the Atlantic and explore Canada's mainland by the temptation of furs, it was whales that led many of them into the northern oceans. In the eighteenth century the British whaling industry was dominated by Hull, but by the middle of the nineteenth Peterhead was the major whaling port in the British Isles. The abundance of whales in Arctic waters had been noted in the earliest voyages north, but until well into the nineteenth century whaling ships that penetrated through Davis Strait, between Greenland and Baffin Island, cautiously hugged the Greenland coast. But gradually Scottish whalers grew familiar with the hazards of Arctic voyaging, and Aberdeen, Dundee and Leith also became important whaling ports. On the way north many ships stopped at Stromness, where they were in the habit of recruiting, often by means of a notice nailed to the door of the parish church. Orkneymen were not only a significant presence on the northern land frontier, but on the ocean frontier also.

The whalers took advantage of the brief Arctic summer to pursue their search for whales. If they were lucky the animals were plentiful and they escaped the Arctic before the return of the ice. The demand for whale bone (baleen) and whale oil was such that it was worth taking risks: the risks became greater when the whalers ventured further north and west. There was increasing pressure to seek out new discoveries. Sometimes these were rediscoveries, as when Captain William Penny, on the *Bon Accord* out of Aberdeen, rediscovered in 1840 Cumberland Sound, unvisited since 1585 when John Davis had first entered it.

William Penny made a number of voyages, contributing, as he searched for whales, to the knowledge of the sounds and inlets of Baffin Island. It was important to understand not only the contours of the coast but also the behaviour of the weather, and especially of the ice. It was meticulous observation of this kind that had led to a renewal of efforts to find a route linking the northern Atlantic and the northern Pacific.

In 1817 William Scoresby, a Whitby whaler who studied with Professor Jameson at Edinburgh University, wrote a letter to Sir Joseph Banks, President of the Royal Society. He reported that conditions in the Arctic, being unusually free of ice, were favourable for further exploration. The letter was passed on to Lord Melville (himself a Scot), First Lord of the Admiralty, who within three weeks had ordered four ships to be fitted out for an expedition. Two ships were to enter Davis Strait and work their way through the maze of straits and islands and inlets and the delusions of ice and fog that lay to the west. The other two ships were to head for the North Pole via Spitzbergen, almost due north of Shetland.

The two ships going west were the *Isabella* and the *Alexander*, under the command of John Ross, son of a Church of Scotland minister. Ross's naval career had begun at the age of ten. During the war with the French he was wounded fourteen times and captured three times: he was a man of considerable experience of hardship.

The objective of the expedition now underway was to chart a passage from east to west: the search for the fabled Northwest Passage, which had been pursued since the sixteenth century, was on again. It was hoped that if Ross sailed into the Davis Strait he would sail out again and on westwards to Kamchatka and ultimately Hawaii.

The voyage was in some respects a disappointment. Ross made his way north following the Greenland coast, escorted by a large fleet of whalers. Having named Melville Bay (Greenland), he turned westward and entered Lancaster Sound, north of Baffin Island, at the end of August. It was late in the season to continue in those waters, but Ross's conviction that Lancaster Sound was closed off by mountains was much criticised: it is in fact the beginning of the way through to the Beaufort Sea.

If Ross's failure to sail through Lancaster Sound was seen by some as faint-hearted, it was the first voyage of a period of intense activity in Arctic waters. In that activity Scots played a leading role. In Ross's wake, literally, came whalers, encouraged to extend their hunting grounds. The Arctic was now being seen less as a means to an end, a quick route to the Far East, and more in terms of its potential value. There was an increasing scientific interest, and men eager to pursue enquiry. And, with the wars with France at an end, there was a sophisticated British navy and aspiring officers whose chances for promotion had been jeopardised by peace, in need of being kept occupied.

In 1819 a more ambitious expedition was planned. It was a two-pronged venture, again initiated by the Admiralty. In May two ships, the *Hecla* and the *Griper,* sailed from Deptford, commanded by William Edward Parry, who had captained the *Alexander* on Ross's expedition. With him on board the *Hecla* was a young man who had served as midshipman of the *Isabella,* James Ross, John Ross's nephew. Eleven days later the Hudson's Bay Company's vessel, the *Prince of Wales,* left Deptford. On board were three men who would become key figures in the exploration of the Arctic: John Franklin, George Back, and Dumfries-born surgeon and naturalist John Richardson.

Parry sailed through Lancaster Sound and reached the south-western tip of Melville Island before ice turned him back. James Ross made important magnetic and meteorological observations, and surgeon-naturalist Alexander Fisher, who had also served on the *Alexander,* collected zoological and geological material. Some of this was donated to the Natural History Museum in Professor Jameson's care at Edinburgh. In the meantime an extraordinary journey on land was being accomplished. From York Factory on Hudson Bay Franklin, the thirty-two year old Richardson, Lieutenant George Back and other members of the expedition covered 8855 km (5,500 miles) by land, lake and river with the object of exploring the continent's Arctic coast.

This gruelling journey took them to Lake Athabasca, north to the Great Slave Lake, and on to the Arctic coast where they explored the area between the mouth of the Coppermine and Turnagain Point on the Kent Peninsula. With winter approaching and provisions short, they had to abandon their damaged canoes and head inland. There followed a journey of extreme hardship, during which ten of the party died of starvation and one, Robert Hood, was shot by an Indian guide. The guide, in his turn, was despatched by a shot in the head from Richardson. There was little to eat apart from lichen scraped from trees. The weather was savage.

Richardson and Franklin had separated during the return journey, with Franklin going on ahead in an effort to reach Fort Enterprise, on the watershed between the Coppermine and Yellowknife Rivers, where promised supplies should have awaited them. But Fort Enterprise was empty, and Franklin's party barely survived, weak and desperate, on boiled shreds of animal hide and lichen. When Richardson reached him he was appalled, although he must himself have presented an equally terrible sight.

> No words can convey an idea of the filth and wretchedness that met our eyes on looking around. Our own misery had stolen on us by degrees, and we were accustomed to the contemplation of each other's emaciated figures, but the ghastly countenances, dilated eyeballs, and sepulchral voices of Captain Franklin and those with him were more than we at first could bear.

In spite of his own extreme weakness, it was Richardson who rallied the party, attended the sick, collected fuel and such scanty food as could be scraped from the trees. There were two further deaths after Richardson's arrival. There is no doubt that they could all have died if it had not been for the appearance of a band of Copper Indians with venison.

The geographical achievement of this, the first of Franklin's expeditions in the Arctic, was remarkable. In addition there was a vast increase in scientific knowledge of the Arctic, and this was largely due to the efforts of John Richardson. Richardson had studied and worked in Dumfries and Edinburgh before becoming a naval surgeon in 1807. He saw service in the French and American wars, continuing his studies as he could in London and Edinburgh, where he gained his MD. He set up practice in Leith, at 36 Constitution Street. While in Edinburgh and Leith, Richardson studied natural history with Professor Jameson, whose considerable reputation and influence had helped to make Edinburgh a focal point of natural science.

Richardson clearly had both an affinity and a talent for the subject. He was also a man of practical good sense. If he were not to remain as a general practitioner, working competitively for a modest income, he had to take advantage of other opportunities that might come up. Britain was at peace and there was a large navy for a range of duties that could bring untold benefits to a nation with worldwide ambitions. The voyages of Captain Cook in the previous century had convinced both government and scientific bodies of the value of exploration and its accompanying sciences: charting, hydrography, geology, meteorology, botany and zoology. The age of the professional scientist was only just beginning, but a growing enthusiasm for scientfic enquiry was to attract many into new areas of interest.

Richardson obtained his qualifications in the city that had the greatest medical reputation in the world. From Edinburgh Scottish doctors took their skills all over the world. Many of them, like Richardson, studied with Jameson and took with them also a keenness that would contribute to the growing knowledge of the natural world. In 1819 Richardson heard that Franklin was preparing an overland expedition. He applied to join. Without his training as a naturalist Richardson might well have been overlooked, for the navy's expeditions needed men who could combine medical and zoological skills.

The part that Richardson played in his first, and most desperate,

Franklin's 'second journey to the shores of the Polar Sea'. On the Mackenzie River, 6th August 1825. Drawn by E N Kendall, a member of the party. (NMS)

expedition cannot be overestimated. Not only did he help to keep the survivors alive by attending to their morale as well as to their physical well-being — he was a convinced Christian — but even in the most extreme conditions he never lost sight of his role as scientific collector and observer. His achievement is reflected in Franklin's narrative of the expedition published in 1823, a considerable part of which was written by Richardson himself. In seven chapters and appendices he wrote up his observations on the natural history of the Arctic. Some of the material Richardson described came to Edinburgh University's Natural History Museum, and are now in the collections of the National Museums of Scotland. This was the first phase of Richardson's extensive zoological publication.

By the time Richardson was again in the Arctic, between 1825 and 1827, he had been recognised as the major natural historian of the region. This second expedition, again with Franklin, proved less drastic that the first. Assistant naturalist was the young botanist Thomas Drummond from Midlothian, 'the most indefatigable collector of specimens' as Richardson described him. He went on to explore and collect in the Rocky Mountains, providing material for Glasgow Botanic Garden and for W J Hooker's *Flora Boreali Americani* (1829-40).

From the second Franklin expedition came back not only natural history material but highly important observations on topology, geology, meteorology, solar radiation and magnetic variations. Richardson's contribution was again crucial. In 1821 Parry had also embarked on another Arctic trip, this time with the *Hecla* and the *Fury*. Once more James Ross was on board, specifically as naturalist, with responsibility not only for collecting material but for stuffing animals and birds. In July 1823 he shot a particularly attractive gull, with a rosy-pink breast. The bird, type specimen of the Roseate or Ross's Gull, was sent, along with other material from the voyage, to Edinburgh where Richardson wrote up the zoological specimens for the account of Parry's second voyage.

There was no question of the invaluable nature of Richardson's contribution to Arctic zoology, but he himself was modest about his achievements, and this was characteristic. He was not only an acknowledged success as explorer and naturalist; his continuing medical career led to his appointment as Physician to the Fleets at the Royal Naval Hospital, Haslar, and in this post he introduced important innovations in nursing and the treatment of the mentally ill. His calm and practical personality impressed many, and he was widely respected. His own muted self-appraisal cannot disguise his distinction. He himself would probably have been happy with the description 'Dr Richardson, the intrepid and intelligent traveller', but he was a great deal more than that, and the modesty of his own words describing his work in the Arctic is misleading.

> ... I had to travel over a country reaching from the great American lakes to the islands of the Arctic Sea, and embracing more than a fourth of the distance from the equator to the pole, which had never before been visited by a professed naturalist. I perceived at once the magnitude of the field, and comprehended at a glance that it was far beyond my grasp. The only previous training I had was the little natural science that I had learned at my northern Alma Mater as a collateral branch of my medical education, but I thought that I could at least record what I saw; and I determined so to do as intelligently as I could and without exaggeration, hoping in this way to furnish facts on which the leaders of science might reason, and thus promote the progress of Natural History to the extent of my limited ability. This was the rule that I followed during the eight years that I passed in those countries actually engaged in the several expeditions.

Richardson did not see himself as a leader of science, yet his contribution to the understanding of the Arctic was invaluable.

Twenty eight years after John Richardson accompanied Franklin on that first expedition he would return to the Arctic to search the coast between the Mackenzie and the Coppermine for some trace of this man who had become one of his closest friends. In that time there had been several government-sponsored expeditions and whalers had become increasingly venturesome, sometimes with dangerous consequences. In 1836 James Ross commanded HMS *Cove* on a mission to rescue whalers trapped in the ice. He was described as 'the finest officer I have ever met with, the most persevering indefatigable man you can imagine'. James Ross is most remembered now for his later Antarctic expedition, but he received his education in the Arctic, and in doing so not only made a profound impression on officers and crew alike, but made a distinctive contribution to geographical and scientific knowledge.

In 1829 the two Rosses, uncle and nephew, began another search for the Northwest Passage. Their four year absence caused considerable worry, but in fact during the ice-bound winters they made several overland journeys, with James Ross locating the Magnetic Pole on 1st June 1831. They had to abandon their ship, the *Victory* to the ice, and made on amazing journey in small boats eastward back

The *Victory,* Sir John Ross's ship on his second Arctic voyage, here seen under sail for the last time before being abandoned to the ice in September 1831. (NMS)

to Lancaster Sound where they were picked up by a whaler who assured them that the Rosses were dead.

Throughout the first half of the nineteenth century the Hudson's Bay Company continued their vital supply trips between the Bay and London. Often these were hazardous. The Company also initiated expeditions which gradually pieced together knowledge of the vast wilderness to the north and west and established the outposts that were often the first step towards settlement. The Hudson's Bay Company merged with the North West Company in 1821, and seven years later George Simpson, born on the shore of Loch Broom in Wester Ross, became Governor in Chief of the Hudson Bay territories. For thirty years this rigorous Scot dominated the Company, and it was his co-operation, with the provision of men, expertise and supply points, that made many government expeditions possible. The recruitment of Scots to the Company was as strong as ever, and many of them made significant contributions to knowledge of the territories as well as furthering the Company's commercial influence. One of these was George Simpson's nephew Thomas who, with Peter Warren Dease, led the Company's expedition of 1837-9 to explore stretches of the Arctic coast west of the Mackenzie and then east of Turnagain Point, which Franklin and Richardson had previously reached.

Scots were coming into Canada in increasing numbers. Although Lord Selkirk's attempt in 1803 to establish a colony on the Red River in what is now Manitoba had not succeeded, later ventures such as the Ayrshire novelist John Galt's Canada Company, which flourished in the 1820s and 30s, encouraged the flow of Scottish immigration. While Scots contributed to the country's development in industry and communications, they continued to be tempted by the frontier, and the frontier continued to need men of endurance and enterprise. Many of them were of heroic stature, and of these perhaps Robert Campbell was typical.

> Robert Campbell was a natural leader of men. His tall commanding figure, sedate bearing, and yet shrewd and adaptable manner, singled him out as one of the remarkable class of men who in the service of the Hudson's Bay Company governed an empire by their personal magnetism, and held many thousands of Indians in check by their honesty, tact, and firmness . . .

Campbell is remembered particularly for his explorations on the Upper Yukon, where Mount Campbell is named after him.

The employees of the Hudson's Bay Company were much more than fur traders, and to be successful explorers they had to have not only courage but diplomacy. Their knowledge of the Indian way of life and of the languages they spoke was often a key to survival, and Scots seemed to have a particular sensitivity in this area. Campbell's adaptability was remarked on. Richardson, too, had the ability to respond positively to the people and circumstances he encountered. Another Company employee, Robert Macfarlane from Stornoway turned this talent to good account and developed a keen interest in the lives of the Athabaskan Indians and Eskimos he encountered. He collected artefacts that illustrated their material culture which through a well-forged chain of initiatives stemming from Edinburgh were sent back to the city's newly established Industrial Museum, and are now amongst the most valued items in the National Museums of Scotland ethnographic collection. He also found the opportunity to collect, observe and publish notes on the mammals and birds of northern Canada.

A picture of the Arctic was taking shape, and for half a century Scots took a lead in filling in the details. Complementing the official government expeditions were the ventures that stemmed from private enterprise. Both depended on the initiative and endurance of individuals. The story of Scottish achievement on the Arctic frontier suggests over and over again a particular combination of qualities. The need for courage and stamina in a land where the terrain, the weather and the people could all present challenges that to most of us would seem to require a superhuman response almost goes without saying. What is striking about the Scottish contribution is an extraordinary independence and sense of purpose, and a commitment that has the steel-edged quality of faith, religious or otherwise. Supporting these were undercurrents of personal loyalty and private glory, both often apparently stronger than any sense of national achievement. Whether these qualities were present in the crewmen of the whaling ships and in the often unwilling pioneer settlers and the other forgotten men and women who confronted the wilderness is impossible to say. But what is clear is that many of the outstanding individuals came from modest, often humble, backgrounds, with little hint that their names would be immortalised on the map of the Arctic regions.

In 1845 Franklin sailed again for the Arctic. Richardson did not accompany him: he was 48 years old, and his first wife had recently died. But when after a year there was no news of Franklin except for

The Arctic Council of 1851. Sir John Richardson is standing pointing to the chart with James Clark Ross fourth from left. The portrait on the left is of Sir John Franklin. Engraving after the painting by Stephen Pearce. (Courtesy of the Scott Polar Research Institute, Cambridge)

that brought back by two Peterhead whalers who had entertained him to dinner in Melville Bay in July 1845, Richardson's voice was one of the strongest to put the case for a search expedition. In the summer of 1848 John Richardson, by now knighted, was once again on the Arctic coast, searching for his friend along stretches between the Mackenzie and the Coppermine that they had once traversed together. With him was John Rae, an employee of the Hudson's Bay Company, who had been the first to explore the west coast of the Melville Peninsula, surveying nearly 1130 km (700 miles) of coastline. Rae, sixteen years Richardson's junior, was born in Stromness and had also studied medicine at Edinburgh. In 1833 he was appointed surgeon to the Hudson's Bay Company. He was another example of a man of many more talents than his medical training might suggest. It is clear that, even measured against other Scottish explorers, he was a man of unusual self-sufficiency and enviable stamina. Whatever his value to the Company as a surgeon, and later as a chief trader, his achievement as an explorer and scientific observer outweighed it.

Rae and Richardson got on very well, and Richardson, now in his fifties, must have been thankful for the assistance and companionship of an experienced younger man. He had, in fact, picked Rae himself, having read about his activities. But even with two such exceptional men, one of whom knew Franklin well and could have best anticipated his movements, there was no success. In 1849 Richardson returned to England, leaving Rae to resume the search. Rae's achievement as an Arctic traveller was due at least in part again to adaptability. He journeyed as the Eskimos journeyed, carrying with him a minimum of equipment and living off the land. In this way he could move fast, and his skill as a hunter ensured he did not starve.

Rae's explorations continued, pushing the frontier northwards. In the winter of 1853-4 he was in Repulse Bay, to the north of Hudson Bay, with the objective of completing the survey of the north coast of America. He crossed the Rae Isthmus by sledge in the spring of 1854, and it was in Pelly Bay that he heard from Eskimos news of the Franklin expedition. The Eskimos reported that some years before they had seen first a party of men heading south from somewhere. north of King William Island, then later about thirty corpses west of Back River. They had relics taken from the corpses, which Rae purchased. This was the first definite news of Franklin and it was on this basis that Rae claimed and received the award of £10,000 that had been offered for information about his fate. Rae spent part of this reward on building and fitting out a schooner for further survey work, but she was lost in a storm.

Undeterred Rae's explorations continued, and included completing surveys for the construction of the telegraph from England and America, via the Faroes, Iceland and Greenland, and another telegraph survey from Winnipeg across the Rockies to the Pacific. Amongst many illustrations of his extraordinary physical stamina was the occasion he walked 64 km (40 miles) in snowshoes in seven hours, from Hamilton to Toronto, and 'dined out the same evening showing no signs of fatigue'. It must have seemed like a stroll compared with some of his Arctic experiences.

Of all the Scots in the Arctic, Rae gives the impression of being not just self-sufficient and independent, but idiosyncratic. He gave thirty years of his life to exploring and increasing the understanding of the northern part of the American continent with an intensity and single-mindedness that probably has no rival. For the remaining thirty years of his life he was based in London, but equally dedicated to furthering the interests of Canada and the Arctic. He lies buried in St Magnus Cathedral, Kirkwall, the most distinguished of the many Orkneymen whose lives are woven into the history of the Arctic lands and oceans.

Like Richardson, John Rae died in England. For most Orcadians, and most Scots, who left their country, whether forced by circumstance or drawn by dreams of a better life, there was little chance of returning to a profitable existence in Scotland. Writing home during the second of Franklin's expeditions, Richardson confessed to 'that romantic attachment which a Scotchman, in his wanderings, feels towards the land of his birth . . .' He was wintering at Fort Franklin on Bear Lake, deep in the wilderness. But it was comfortable, the log cabins warm and weatherproof, game plentiful, and fish remarkably large — he mentions trout of up to 22 kg (50 pounds) each. There were about fifty men, women and children at Fort Franklin, and most of the men were Scottish. Amongst them were a piper and a fiddler. The Scots became renowned throughout the world for transplanting their culture. It perhaps made it easier to accept exile, and perhaps contributed as much as dogged Christianity, astute commercialism and toughness of constitution to their achievement in the unwelcoming Arctic.

Thomas Lipton, Glasgow provision merchant, cornered one tenth of the tea trade in the late 19th century. Although the Northwest Passage proved to be no shortcut to Asia Scots were active in Eastern commerce. Scots were leaders in the development of tea plantations in India, and built and manned many of the clipper ships that brought tea to Britain. Scottish exports to the East illustrate another facet of Scottish enterprise. The story of the marketing of Scottish pottery in Southeast Asia is a striking example.

SCOTLAND'S ORIENTAL LINKS: SCOTTISH POTTERY IN SOUTH EAST ASIA

G R Dalgleish

One of the least well documented aspects of Scottish trading enterprise in the nineteenth century must surely be the large-scale export of pottery to all parts of the world. The lack of evidence is especially frustrating when the few glimpses we do have of this trade point to a well run and highly developed business. We know, for example, that in 1867 Scottish ports alone were shipping out £177,547 worth of earthenware and porcelain, while large quantities were also being taken into England by land for subsequent export. Many Scottish potteries seem to have had a flourishing trade with Canada, the USA, the West Indies and the East Indies, and by the second half of the century several had built up complex and extensive business contacts in these areas. The Canadian trade of Robert Cochran's Verreville Pottery in Glasgow was important enough for him to send out one of his assistants to open a warehouse in Montreal to distribute his wares and to expand into the US market.

Considering the obvious importance of this trade it is all the more surprising that, until recently, the only evidence for specialised export ware was in the form of fragmentary sherd material recovered from excavations at pottery waste dumps in Glasgow. This suggested that at least one Glasgow pottery was producing items designed specifically for export to the Far East. The existence of the trade is not in the least unexpected however, considering the extensive nature of other commercial connections between Scotland and the East. These were no doubt started by the large numbers of Scots who sought their fortunes in the East India Company in the late eighteenth century. Such contacts developed with the growth of many Scottish-run agency houses and managing agencies after the Company's monopolies in the Indian and China trades had been broken.

In 1980 a series of happy coincidences combined to produce a partial breakthrough in understanding this hidden aspect of Scotland's entrepreneurial past. The first came when Graeme Cruickshank, who was researching designs registered by Scottish potteries in the Public Record Office in London, discovered a large series of designs for transfer prints with an unmistakeably oriental style, unlike anything known on existing plates. They dated from the mid 1880s to 1906 and were recorded by J & M P Bell & Co Ltd of Glasgow. Unfortunately there was no other information about them. At this point a second discovery provided many of the answers to the questions posed by these enigmatic oriental designs. Many of the actual plates bearing these patterns were found in the bazaars and markets of the area for which they were undoubtedly produced: Java and Sumatra. They were spotted by Edwin Robertson, who was working on an engineering project on the rural water supply in West Java. He recognised the importance of these plates and made an extensive collection before returning to Britain in 1982.

This remarkable collection, from which the National Museum of

Antiquities of Scotland bought a fully representative selection, contained examples of the products of eight separate Scottish potteries: J Marshall & Co, Bo'ness; David Methven & Son, Kirkcaldy; the Clyde Pottery Co, Greenock; and John Thomson & Sons, R A Kidston & Co, David Lockhart & Co, Robert Cochran & Co and J & M P Bell & Co, all of Glasgow. The vast majority of the pieces, however, were made by the last of these, J & M P Bell & Co. In total, this collection gives a fascinating and unique insight into the development of the export trade and suggests that there was a definite pattern and plan behind it.

The earliest dateable plates are decorated with standard transfer printed designs of a type that was common throughout Britain. One of the oldest bears a pattern called 'Victoria Scroll', produced by J & M P Bell & Co, with a registry mark for 1853, while other popular patterns include Bell's 'Harvest' and R A Kidston's beautifully executed 'Syrian'. This last example represents a type of pattern that was strongly featured in the collection, based on stylised 'oriental' designs popular in Britain from the end of the eighteenth and throughout the nineteenth century. The inspiration for these 'oriental' designs was not directly from indigenous motifs, but rather from the many travel books illustrated with much romanticised topographical views. It is somewhat ironic that Britain's potteries were exporting wares with these designs back to the areas which had provided, however remotely, their original inspiration.

Presumably these patterns were popular in the East, for a few of the most enterprising potteries further developed their range to produce designs exclusively for the South East Asian trade. The men who masterminded this export drive were certainly aware of the specialised nature of this market and geared their product accordingly. An astonishing range of designs was developed by several factories, drawing directly on traditional motifs from China, Japan and the Malay-Indonesian Archipelago. Other production factors were also innovations, such as the range of colours used in the prints, hardly any of which could be described as normal by Scottish standards, and the use of two coloured printing, a technique that was extremely rare in Scotland.

The final proof of the commercial ability of the Scottish potters, if any more is needed, must undoubtedly be their use of local scripts for the Trademarks on the plates, presumably to enable local traders and customers who did not speak English to know exactly which patterns they were buying.

Although several Scottish potteries were involved in the eastern trade, one concern really seems to have dominated the scene, demonstrating a quite remarkable degree of business skill and marketing enterprise: the Glasgow Pottery of J & M P Bell. This pottery, at one time the best known in Scotland, was established on the banks of the Forth-Clyde Canal, between St Rollox and Port Dundas in Glasgow, by the brothers John and Matthew Perston Bell. They began manufacturing high quality earthenware in 1842 and by 1847 had moved into the production of china. Within a short period they had mastered the art, and were in fact the only Scottish pottery deemed worthy by the London organisers to exhibit their goods at the Great Exhibition of 1851. Their fine reproduction of the Warwick Vase was singled out for high praise, and certainly this and other pieces exhibited suggest that they were employing very skilled potters and decorators.

'Pekin', pattern by J and M P Bell showing the Temple of the Sun. (NMS)

The Temple of the Sun, Peking, the lower terraces lined with Indian troops from the British force sent to quell the Boxer Rebellion, 1900. (Courtesy of the National Army Museum)

The Bell brothers were obviously accomplished businessmen and grasped early on the importance of the lucrative Far Eastern trade. Their initial printed advertisement stated that they intend to produce their wares for both 'home sale and exportation', and it is clear that they soon built up strong business contacts with the East. John Bell owned a trading company based in Rangoon, ideally situated to keep a finger on the pulse of the Indian, Chinese and East Indian trade routes. In 1880 Dunedin, Bell's property in Rangoon, comprised of warehouses, timber yard and a shipbuilding yard, was valued at £10,000, which included £1,300 for elephants and moveable plant! The company seems to have operated through a system of agents who were established in the main trading centres of the area, including Surabaya, Manila and Batavia. Presumably these agents were used to market the products of the parent pottery company in Scotland.

Bell's commercial links with Batavia provide a vivid illustration of their business acumen and enterprise. Not only had they an agent working for them there, they also named one of the patterns after the town. This may not at first appear exceptional, but we should remember that Batavia was the capital of the Dutch East Indies and therefore, theoretically at least, the trading preserve of the Dutch. One would imagine that this fine example of Scottish 'cheek' might have annoyed the Dutch colonists and local manufacturers alike, since one of the area's staple industries was manufacturing pottery.

Although John Bell laid the foundations of the company's export trade, and built up the necessary commercial infrastructure, it was the men who took over the pottery after his death in March 1880 who brought the specialist export lines to their climax. As John died intestate and with no direct heirs (his brother Matthew pre-deceased him in 1870), his assets were sequestrated, and the pottery — which was valued at about £60,000 — was sold by his trustees to a group of men who set up a joint stock company which traded under the name of J & M P Bell & Co Ltd. The main shareholder and managing director of the new company was James Murdoch, the former works manager under Bell.

It was during the period from the early 1880s to about 1906 that the company produced the most remarkable series of designs specifically for South East Asia. We know of at least 29 designs, all registered with the Patent Office in London, created solely for this purpose. Each pattern was printed in up to eight different colour variations, including two-colour printing.

Many of the pattern titles were taken from local placenames, including Johore, Kalantan, Pekin, Makasser, Banda, Borneo, Celebes, Kwantung and Sumatra. The drawing of the designs suggest that the artists were acquainted with the area and had a more than superficial knowledge of their subjects. The pattern called 'Pekin', for example, depicts a building which must surely be the Temple of the Sun in that city.

Another area in which Bell's led the field was their use of the local language as part of their Trademark. Many of their plates carried the pattern name printed on the back in *Jawi,* a Malay form of Arabic script, and the language spoken by the trading fraternity of the Malay-Indonesian Archipelago.

The evidence of the existing plates suggests that the company must have devoted a major section of their total production capacity to this Oriental trade. It is even possible that they had a complete production line, from initial pattern design to final firing given over entirely to the manufacture of this ware. This, of course, must remain speculation, as there is as yet no way of knowing the total quantities of plates being exported. It is perhaps significant, however, that when comparing the number of specialist eastern designs with the number of patterns produced for the domestic market, we discover that out of a total (domestic and export) of about 70 patterns after 1881, 29 (or 40 per cent) were exclusively for export. Also indicative of the importance to Bell's of this section of production is the fact that export designs form a very high proportion of all the designs which the company registered with the Patent Office. It would seem that they were keen to protect legally these designs against being copied, something they did not necessarily bother with in their domestic ware.

The production seems to have carried on until around 1906, when the fortunes of the Company took a downward turn. The First World War may well have dealt the final blow to an already weakened company, for shortly after this a large part of Bell's factory was bought by the Caledonian Railway Company, who demolished the buildings to make way for the Buchanan Street Goods Station.

The return of this marvellous collection to Scotland has been a major breakthrough in understanding one aspect of our overseas trade. However, it poses as many questions as it has answered. Who, for example, designed the patterns? Arnold Fleming in *Scottish Pottery* (Glasgow, 1923) gives a hint when he states that some 'beautiful patterns were specially designed by Chinese artists'. Unfortunately, he does not go on to say if these artists were resident in Scotland or if the designs were imported from the East. Nor is it known for whom the pottery was made — whether it was the local population or the European colonists. At the Scottish end of the trade route, we do not know which shipping companies transported it to the East, or anything about the financial arrangements. The foregoing summary must therefore be seen as merely a statement of work in progress, as much remains to be done before this remarkable example of Scottish enterprise is fully understood.

NMS

*Although in the 19th century Scotland was trading
energetically in the East it was the commercial possibilities of
the New World that first attracted Scottish merchants to
look beyond Europe. Figures such as this, in the collections of
the National Museums of Scotland, were the emblems of
tobacco sellers. Glasgow merchants participated in the
tobacco trade with the American colonies before the Act of
Union of 1707 allowed legal trading. The trade flourished
through most of the 18th century, and contributed greatly to
Scotland's economic development in general and Glasgow's
expansion in particular. The increase in trade created a
demand for ships, to which Glasgow responded.*

THE SHIPBUILDERS

Anthony Slaven

Building vessels for local trade and fishing was a long established craft in Scotland, but at the beginning of the nineteenth century Scotland had no great reputation as a shipbuilding nation. Numerous small slipways could be found around the coasts and estuaries of the Clyde, Forth, Tay, Dee and Don, but the output of the industry was small, perhaps only some 10,000 tons in 1820 when British building stood at over 66,000 tons. Nearly two-thirds of this Scottish output came from the east coast, and the Clyde was far from being the leading area of construction. Fifty years later the Clyde supplied nearly one-third of all British tonnage, and was then the single most important shipbuilding river in the world, a position it retained down to the First World War. In that short period the industry had been revolutionised; even as traditional building in wood and sail moved to its peak, the new face of shipbuilding, the industry of steam and iron, was being created. The substitution of steam power for wind power, and metal for timber in the construction of hulls, was a long process, and the Scottish contribution to the new industry was striking in invention but even more notable in innovation and enterprise.

The Conquest of Steam

The key event in the development of the modern shipbuilding industry in Scotland is usually seen to be the launching of Henry Bell's *Comet* on the Clyde in 1812, this vessel successfully demonstrating the commercial viability of steam-powered vessels on protected estuaries. But in the 20 years or so before that event there had been two important precursors. The man at the centre of these was William Symington, an engineer who had learned his craft dealing with colliery steam engines. In 1788 he, in association with an Edinburgh banker, Patrick Miller, and another partner James Taylor, designed and sailed a twin-hulled paddle boat on Loch Dalswinton in Dumfriesshire, powered by an atmospheric engine employing a separate condenser. There was no commercial development from this venture but in 1800 Symington was employed by the directors of the Forth and Clyde Canal to experiment with steam power. The result was the *Charlotte Dundas* of 1803, which sailed successfully driving its paddles with a horizontal double-acting single cylinder steam engine. In spite of the fact that the canal directors decided against continuing with steam because of fears of erosion of the canal banks by the waves created, the practicality of the paddle steamer had been demonstrated. Even so, steamship building made no impact on Clyde shipbuilders and shipowners until Henry Bell launched his *Comet*.

In innovating his ferry service with the *Comet* Henry Bell showed the way forward in both the use of steam for powering vessels, and in the technique of successful steamboat building. Bell was an entrepreneur, not a shipbuilder. He saw a commercial opportunity and brought together the ingredients in a successful recipe. While Bell designed the vessel, he did not build it. The hull came from the Port Glasgow yard of John and Charles Wood; the engine was commissioned from John Robertson and constructed in Glasgow at his engineering works in Dempster Street; the boiler was made by David Napier at his Camlachie Foundry. The technique was simple and effective, and was quickly copied not only on the Clyde but on other major shipbuilding rivers, notably the Thames and Mersey.

Although other shipbuilding rivers quickly followed the Clyde's lead, it was Clydeside engineers and boat builders who were the real pioneers in the first decade of steamboat building. Between 1812 and 1820 Clyde builders launched 42 steamboats of over 3,000 grt, some 60 per cent of all steam tonnage built in Britain. The main builders of the new steamboats on the Clyde included John and Charles Wood of Port Glasgow, Archibald McLauchlan of Dumbarton, James Munn of Greenock, John Hunter of Port Glasgow, J W Fife of Fairlie, and William Denny at Dumbarton. None of these men built the engines or the boilers, but fitted them into their modified wooden hulls and relied on a growing number of engine shops and foundries that were turning their attention to the new market. Following in the footsteps of John Robertson and David Napier there came George Dobie, James Cook, and John Thomson, all in the Tradeston district of Glasgow, together with D McArthur close by in Camlachie.

This first exciting phase was very much a trial and error affair, and it soon became clear that if steam was to succeed outside protected estuary service, then marine steam engines had to become more reliable and economic. Moreover marine boilers had to be developed to deliver steam efficiently at higher pressures; an efficient system of propulsion had to be created, and hull forms had to be redesigned and strengthened to cope with the strains imposed upon vessels by the new machinery. Scottish inventiveness made contributions in all four areas, though making its greatest impact in the development of marine steam engines and marine boilers.

Perhaps the most influential family in this pioneering phase was the Napiers. David Napier had supplied the boiler for the *Comet* and rapidly expanded into building the new steam engines. Not satisfied with that, he moved his base from Camlachie to Lancefield, where in 1821 he established a shipyard to link with his own engine work and foundry. He was the first entrepreneur to combine boiler, engine and ship construction in a single business, and consequently he was made aware of the challenges which had to be accepted in order to make the new steamboat a commercial success. He began his attack by focusing on the efficiency of the design of the hull, and between 1818 and 1820 he had tested wooden models in a burn, coming to the view that a wedged shape bow was better for the new paddle boats than the traditional bluff bow of the standard sailing ship. His new design was widely employed.

Important as this was, the redesign of the hull form did not itself solve the problem of economy and use of steam for longer ocean voyages. The early engines consumed coal at alarming rates and the accompanying boilers were only capable of sustaining low pressures of barely two pounds per square inch. The boilers were also likely to explode as the use of sea water to cool the steam in the cylinder developed a concentrated brine in the boiler, corroding and weakening it. Napier attempted to solve this problem by patenting an improved version of James Watt's separate condenser. This device kept the steam in the cylinder and cooling water separate, thus avoiding the danger of corrosion. He was only partially successful in this and effective versions of the separate condenser did not come fully into use until the 1860s.

Simultaneously with his work on the separate condenser David Napier introduced an improved form of engine, his *Steeple* engine of 1835, a more compact design than the more common side-levered versions then in use. His Steeple engine was to become a popular variant for paddle steamers built on the Clyde for the next 30 years. Shortly after, in 1841, he patented an improved version of the feathering paddle, designed to minimise the resistance of the blades on entry to and exit from the water. Sadly, David Napier left the Clyde at the height of his powers, moving to London in 1836. By then he had integrated shipbuilding and marine engineering in one operation; he had achieved considerable economy in boiler and engine design and use, and his vessels had been leaders in hull form and in pioneering open sea routes between Glasgow and Belfast. He had also built the first iron steamer in Scotland, the *Aglaia* of 1827, which plied on Loch Eck.

With David Napier's departure, leadership passed to his cousins James and Robert Napier. In 1835 James Napier developed an improved form of boiler, the Haystack tubular boiler, which passed the hot gases vertically upward through a series of tubes, conserving heat and cutting fuel consumption by up to 30 per cent. This innovation long remained the most popular boiler installed in river steamers. James' brother, Robert Napier, moved into the Camlachie Foundry when David Napier vacated it in 1821 and then opened the Vulcan Foundry close by David Napier's Lancefield Works. These two enterprises, the Lancefield and Vulcan Works, were to be the seedbed for several generations of leading Clyde shipbuilders and marine engineers. David Tod and John MacGregor trained at the Lancefield Works before setting up their own engine works in 1834, and their shipyard in 1836 specifically to build iron vessels. James Thomson managed Robert Napier's Camlachie Foundry from 1828 and then moved to join his brother George to be managers in the Lancefield Works in 1838. The firm of J & G Thomson was founded at Mavisbank in 1847 and ultimately moved to a greenfield site at Clydebank in 1870; the firm eventually was bought out by John Brown & Co in 1899. Among others trained in these works were Charles Randolph, the two Elders, William Pearce, and Dr A C Kirk. The Napier stable also laid the foundation for one of the greatest of Britain's shipping lines, The Cunard Company. Robert Napier was a partner in the founding company in 1839, and designed and engined the first four Cunard liners to ply on the North Atlantic route.

The period from the launching of the *Comet* to the 1850s was the era of the paddle steamer and the Clyde was a great nursery for the engineers and builders who pioneered this revolution. The Napiers were prominent in this, but were not the only contributors. The network of early builders experimented, refined and innovated with each vessel they launched and collectively kept the Clyde in the forefront of steamship building in Britain and hence in the world. After the Clyde's initial lead in the 1810s, other shipbuilding rivers had quickly captured a major share in steamboat building, but by the 1840s the Clyde had recaptured its position of leadership. Two-

Selection of export
plates by J & M P Bell,
showing the eight colour
variations. (NMS)

John Brown's shipyard
today. (NMS)

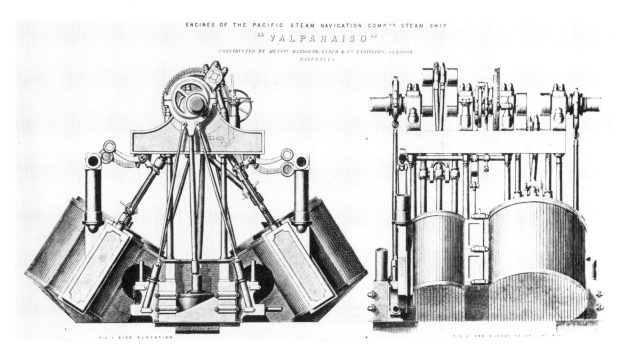

FIG.1 SIDE ELEVATION

FIG.2 END ELEVATION ON LINE A B

thirds of all steam tonnage built in Britain in the 1840s came from the Clyde yards and this was still the position a decade later.

The Clyde's lead in this depended essentially upon a vigorous exploitation of sound engineering applied to the design of boilers and steam engines and linking this to improvements in the paddle wheel. But by 1840 a new prospect for propulsion was under test, the screw propeller. By being totally submerged the screw had an advantage over the paddle, but in order to be efficient it had to revolve at high speeds. In Britain the breakthrough did not come on the Clyde, but in England. Patents were taken variously by Woodcroft in 1826 and 1832, and independently in 1836 by Thomas Smith and John Ericson. Smith's version was the one taken up commercially. In Scotland the first successful demonstration was, like so many of the first steps in Scottish marine engineering, taken on a canal. In 1840 Captain Thomas Kincaid, father of the marine engine builder J G Kincaid of Greenock, conducted experiments with a screw driven steamer on the Forth and Clyde Canal.

By the middle of the nineteenth century the improvements in boilers had raised working pressures from two to forty pounds per square inch, and the developments in the steam engine allied to this were bringing the Atlantic routes within the capacity of the steamer. This longer distance travel was also made more possible with the introduction of the screw propeller. But the regular use of steam on longer routes demanded still greater power and economy. Clydeside engineers were again to solve this problem with the introduction of the compound expansion marine steam engine. This innovation came from Charles Randolph and John Elder in 1853, when they installed their improved engine in the *SS Brandon*. In their compound engine the power of the steam was not squandered in one cylinder but was expanded successively in two cylinders, first in a high pressure cylinder followed then by expansion in a low pressure cylinder. This delivered economies of about one-third over normal

SS *Valparaiso*. Randolph & Elder's Compound marine engine revolutionised the economy of steam for longer voyages. The drawings show the high and low pressure cylinders. (By kind permission of University of Glasgow Archives)

fuel consumption in the single cylinder engines then popularly in use. Charles Randolph had trained as an engineer in Robert Napier's works at Camlachie under David Elder, John Elder's father. The young Elder also trained with his father and joined with Randolph in partnership in 1852 to form Randolph Elder and Company. Their innovation was in such demand that they themselves established a shipyard in 1858 to exploit it, and by 1864 they built a new yard at Fairfield Farm, Govan, the company eventually becoming the Fairfield Shipbuilding and Engineering Co. The yard survives today as the solitary merchant yard on the Upper Clyde, operating within British Shipbuilders as Govan Shipbuilders.

This dramatic innovation called for yet higher steam pressures from the boilers to deliver full efficiency. The solution came from yet another Glasgow engineer, James Howden. The quest for very high boiler pressures led design away from early box or tank types to experimentation with cylindrical forms in which the water was contained in a complex honeycomb of pipes around which the hot combustion gases circulated. The principle had long been known, but early efforts were not very successful until James Howden introduced his cylindrical version which became known as the 'Scotch' boiler. When linked to the forced draught which had been patented by David Napier in 1851, and combined with the strength of steel plates, this boiler delivered the very high pressures required to guarantee the economies inherent in Randolph and Elder's compound steam engine.

From this innovation it was a short logical step to yet further savings in expanding the power of steam in more than two cylinders. There is some suggestion that the Clyde yard of Thomas Wingate & Co built a triple expansion engine in 1872, but the available evidence points to the breakthrough being in 1874 when Dr A C Kirk, of John Elder & Co, developed this new engine. His triple expansion engine was installed in the SS Propontis. Somewhat surprisingly the new triple expansion engine was only linked to the power of the Scotch boiler in 1881 when Kirk installed it in the Aberdeen for George Thomson's Aberdeen Line for the long Australian route.

The longest sea voyages were now within the compass of the steamship. Compound and triple expansion engines had delivered great economies and the Clydeside engineers continued their search in this direction. In 1884 Walter Brock, a nephew and partner to Peter Denny, introduced his quadruple expansion engine in which the power of the steam was released in four successive stages of expansion. This was a more complex and expensive engine than the triple expansion version and was used mainly for the largest cargo vessels. It was A C Kirk's triple expansion engine which remained the most effective and popular version of the reciprocating marine steam engine and which retained world leadership in marine engineering for the Clyde in the second half of the nineteenth century.

These innovations in boilers and in marine steam engines stressed economy of fuel rather than speed. Greater speeds were achieved by installing twin and triple screws driven by separate engines, and by improving the balancing of engines to reduce vibration. But even such refinements could not overcome the main weakness of the reciprocating engine. There was always a loss of power and efficiency in converting the up and down motion of the reciprocating engine into the rotary motion necessary to drive the screws. The solution was to devise an engine capable of transmitting rotary motion direct to the screws. This was achieved with the development of the steam turbine, patented in Britain in 1894 by Charles Parsons. In contrast to the reciprocating engine, which could not deliver high enough speeds to the screw, the turbine, in a direct acting form, transmitted very high revolutions and required a system of reduction gearing to be developed to deliver the most economical speeds between turbine and screw revolutions.

While the turbine was not developed on the Clyde, its commercial innovation came there in 1901. William Denny and Bros joined with Charles Parsons and a shipowner, Captain John Williamson, to form the Turbine Steam Syndicate. The result was Denny's construction of the *King Edward,* the world's first turbine-powered merchant ship. The Dennys moved swiftly into the building of turbine-driven ships and were followed in 1905 by A & J Inglis who were the first Clyde yard to negotiate a Parsons' licence. The first direct acting turbines had to be worked well below full efficiency because of the slower speeds required by the screw propellers. The answer was reduction gearing and by 1912 the Fairfield Yard had built the first two vessels with geared turbine machinery. The Clyde also developed an alternative form of the turbine on the basis of the version developed in the United States by Curtis. John Brown & Co of Clydebank negotiated a licence on the basis of which the Brown-Curtis turbine was developed, partly with the assistance of Professor Sir John G Biles, then Professor of Naval Architecture at Glasgow University.

The development of the steam turbine brought the conquest of steam to its fullest development on the Clyde. Clydeside engineers and shipbuilders had either introduced or quickly innovated every major stage in the search for economy and efficiency in the development of marine steam engines and boilers. The tradition and reputation of the Scots engineer had been stamped across the world's trade routes by vessels pouring from the Clyde's slipways. The challenge of the motor vessel was yet only dimly on the horizon, and even there the Clyde shipbuilders built and launched the second largest ocean-going motor ship in the world, the *Jutlandia.* This was built by Barclay Curle & Co as one of a pair ordered by the Danish shipping company, the East Asiatic Co. While this engine was not in the main line of Clydeside Engineering tradition, it was quickly taken up and before the First World War the Glasgow engine works of Harland & Wolff were the largest producers of diesel engines in the world. They built the diesel to the licence of the Danish company of Burmeister and Wain. At least until the First World War, there was no sign of any flagging in Scottish enterprise and innovation in the challenge of marine engineering and shipbuilding.

Iron and Steel

The innovation of steam engines placed great strains on the wooden hulls of vessels and stimulated a search for a stronger alternative form of construction. The obvious answer was the use of iron. An iron barge had been built by the English iron master John Wilkinson in 1787 for canal use. This experiment was repeated in Scotland in 1818 when another canal barge, the *Vulcan,* was constructed by Thomas Wilson at his works at Faskine on the Monkland Canal. The *Vulcan* plied on the Forth and Clyde Canal as a passenger vessel till 1873. It was the world's first iron passenger vessel and was a significant development in a number of ways. In design it introduced angle irons, vertical strakes or ribs, and the use of two-ply rivetted iron plates. Iron hulls were clearly practicable and the next stage was to link iron to steam power. This came in Scotland in 1827 when the redoubtable David Napier build his vessel the *Aglaia*, quickly followed in 1831 by John Neilson with his *Fairy Queen*, the first iron paddle steamer to ply on the Clyde. Four years later Tod and MacGregor from their new shipyard launched the *Loch Goil*. Other builders followed and by 1840 Clyde-built iron steamers were making open sea voyages.

The pressures to use iron in construction grew in intensity as the power of the steam engines developed, and as shipowners asked for ever larger vessels to carry cargo more economically. The early and slow revolving paddles had placed little strain on wooden hulls but as speeds grew, vibration increased and weakened the hull. Moreover, as wooden hulls approached 300 feet in length, timber tended to lose its strength and rigidity in construction. Even so iron was only adopted slowly and very few iron vessels were constructed before 1845. However, once the screw propeller began to be adopted, the advantages of the strength of iron became more obvious, and the Clyde shipbuilders paralleled the enterprise of the Clydeside engineers in pioneering construction. As a consequence virtually all the iron tonnage built in Britain in the 1840s came from the River Clyde, and for 20 years from 1851 to 1870 the Clyde yards supplied over 70 per cent of all iron tonnage launched in Britain. By 1870, 90 per cent of all vessels built on the Clyde were of iron.

This pioneering development of the use of iron in constructing the hulls of vessels also encouraged innovation in the design and testing of the hulls and bow forms. This focus on design and upon naval architecture came from a long tradition of experimentation which can be traced to David Napier's early trials to develop a wedge-shaped bow for paddle steamers between 1818 and 1820. Perhaps the most significant early contribution from this type of experimentation came from the work of John Scott Russell. Russell's experiments were, like so many others in Scotland, carried out upon a canal, this time on the Union Canal. Russell was engaged to experiment with the design of vessels to minimise the effect of waves from the bows upon the canal banks. In experimenting in this area of hydro-dynamics, Russell discovered in 1834 the phenomenon of the single wave: the continuous wave set in motion by the ship's bow had particular forms depending upon the shape of the hull and the speed of the vessel. From this emerged the theory of the 'wave form' for the design of hulls. Russell became manager at Thomson and Speirs' yard in Greenock, remaining there as manager when the yard was taken over by Caird & Co; he then went to England in 1844 where he was to be the designer and builder of Isambard Kingdom Brunel's *Great Eastern*, the largest vessel in the world at that time.

Scott Russell's influence on ship design had wide repercussions; in addition to developing the wave form theory for hull design, he evolved the principle of longitudinal bracing in the construction of iron ships, an innovation soon copied on the Clyde. While this type of enquiry was uncommon, given its scientific dimension, it was not unique on the Clyde. Among many others who contributed to the theory of testing and to the design of iron vessels, the young William Denny, son of Dr Peter Denny of Dumbarton, was particularly notable. William Denny was an experimental scientist of some distinction and worked with the influential naval architect, Dr William

Froude. Froude persuaded the Admiralty that good ship design required effective testing of models, and under his direction Britain's first full-scale test tank was built at Torquay in 1872. William Denny had worked for a time as his assistant, and by 1883 he had persuaded his father to build the first test tank in a commercial shipyard anywhere in Britain. Under William Denny's influence, the company also pioneered the construction of double cellular bottoms for cargo vessels. There was a deep commitment to experimentation and innovation on the Clyde in the nineteenth century and this found expression in 1881 in the founding of a lectureship in Naval Architecture in the University of Glasgow. Two years later, in 1883, through a generous endowment from Mrs Elder, the widow of John Elder, the Elder Chair of Naval Architecture was established. This was the first such chair anywhere in the world.

The conquest of steam and iron had propelled the Clyde from obscurity to world leadership in shipbuilding by the 1870s. But impressive as the achievements of these years were, they were to be surpassed between 1880 and 1913. During this period the Clyde consistently built and launched more than one-third of all British tonnage; in 1913 with an output of 756,973 grt, the Clyde delivered

The elegant saloon of the *City of Paris,* one of the earliest steel vessels (1880s), showing that the Clyde-built reputation rested on craftsmanship as well as marine engineering and naval architecture. (By kind permission of University of Glasgow Archives)

18 per cent of all the world tonnage. This spectacular achievement was built not only upon the skill of Clydeside marine engineering, but on the entrepreneurship of the builders who, having barely established iron as the material capable of supporting the development of larger and faster vessels, turned their attention to steel. The Scottish steel industry was developing rapidly in the 1870s and the early steel plates attracted the attention of the Clyde shipbuilders, even then in search of greater strength, flexibility and lightness in their building materials. Steel was superior to iron in these qualities, and the Clyde anticipated the rush to use steel in a series of successful pioneer vessels in the 1870s.

John Elder & Co launched two steel paddle steamers in 1877, and in 1879 William Denny & Co launched the *Rotomahana,* which can claim to be the world's first ocean-going vessel of any size to be constructed entirely in mild steel. Two years later the Clydebank company of J & G Thomson launched the *Servia,* the first Cunarder to be built of steel. At this stage, 1881, the Clyde was building only ten per cent of its tonnage in the new material; but by 1884 nearly half of all Clyde-built vessels were of steel, and by 1889 iron had virtually disappeared as a constructional material with mild steel reigning supreme. The Clyde had led the revolution in building in iron, and repeated its leadership with steel. 'Clyde built' had come to represent the stamp of quality, reliability, and pride in achievement of Scottish building.

The Shipbuilders

Who were the men who accomplished the transformation of shipbuilding from a small scale craft in wood and sail to the large scale heavy engineering assembly trade in steam and steel? At first sight there have been an astonishing number of companies building vessels from the smallest barges to the largest liners and warships, some 250 in all in operation at one time or another during the nineteenth century. Most of these were small and short-lived, but from within this galaxy there emerged the winners, those with the skill, the stamina, and the determination to build a lasting reputation.

At Greenock the most significant group of builders included Scott's established in 1711, the oldest shipbuilding company in the world. Robert Duncan & Co from 1830 and Caird & Co from 1840. At Port Glasgow building was dominated by Russell & Co from 1867 and ultimately by Lithgows. Across the river, Dumbarton was another early centre of construction, where two firms in particular had a great life span, namely, Denny of Dumbarton from 1818 and Archibald McMillan & Son from 1834. While the earliest building took place on the lower Clyde, the Glasgow area began to develop rapidly with the deepening of the river from the 1830s. Robert Napier & Sons was established in 1836, as was Tod & MacGregor whose yard was eventually taken over by D & W Henderson from 1873. J & G Thomson set up at Mavisbank in 1847, and moved to Clydebank in 1870. In 1845 the firm of Barclay Curle & Co was established, though John Barclay had been building at Stobcross since 1818. Neilson & Co set up at Whiteinch in 1850, and in 1858 Randolph & Elder began building vessels. This company passed to John Elder & Co in 1870, eventually becoming the Fairfield Shipbuilding & Engineering Co from 1886. The Stephens came to the Clyde in 1851 after a century of building on the north-east coast at

Aberdeen and Arbroath. A decade later Charles Connell established his own yard at Scotstoun.

Most of the famous shipyards and shipbuilding companies were being formed on the Clyde around the middle decades of the nineteenth century, though three of the best known were later incomers. John Brown & Co bought into Clydebank in 1899, Harland and Wolff of Belfast set up on the Clyde in 1912 and Yarrow & Co moved from the Thames to the Clyde in 1906.

The names and the families associated with them are familiar, but little in detail is known about these men. What was their background and how did they get into the business? How were they trained and what contribution did they as individuals make to the development of a great industry and to the reputation of 'Clyde built'? Were they really great men, or simply men in the right place at the right time, men who succeeded in one set of circumstances, but who might just as easily have failed if circumstances had been different? Research into the lives of these men now allows us to offer some view on these questions.

Although there had been some building of ships on the Clyde since the Scotts established their yard at Greenock in 1711, the first opportunity for a more extensive industry came in the pioneering years of steam. Between 1812 and the 1830s most of the new firms drew their men from one of two sources. The new shipbuilders in steam either came from some of the early firms of wood builders like John & Charles Wood and John McLauchlan, or from the engineering works of families like the Napiers and the Neilsons. Many of the leading firms began in this way and it is clear that, in the later years of the nineteenth century, the leading shipbuilders were largely sons, grandsons, cousins or nephews of the founding families. Consequently, by the end of the century, it is the third generation of Dennys who are in control at Dumbarton. Similarly, it is the fifth generation of the Stephens who were building at Linthouse. When William Tod Lithgow died as a founding partner of Russell & Co, his interest passed to his two sons, James and Henry. Within the great company of Barclay & Curle, the position of managing director ultimately passed from father to son, being handed on from Archibald Gilchrist to James. Similar patterns of preferment can be found in virtually every company. Given this pattern it is also clear that relatively few men rose to the top positions in any of the shipbuilding firms in Clydeside if they were not within the family network.

When some such men did aspire to partnership position it was usually through the death of a family line leaving no one to fill the position in management and ownership. Sir William Pearce rose to control John Elder & Co after Elder's early death in 1869. The two other partners in the concern were unable to carry the management on their own and took him in to provide much needed skills. Similarly, Dr A C Kirk rose to be the head of the great firm of Robert Napier after Napier's death. In both cases these men came into positions of senior control and ownership in companies which combined several families in partnership. Single family structured firms, like the Stephens, or the Dennys, were much tighter in family network control, and in the nineteenth century the partnership door in these firms remained tightly closed to non-family personnel. This exclusion related only to the boardroom; the family firms, like all of the others on the Clyde, regularly employed able and experienced men as managers in their engine shops, design offices and shipyards.

While in later years the family and partnership network largely controlled access to senior executive position in the Clydeside companies, it is apparent that in the initial founding of these companies many of the men had little or no previous experience of shipbuilding. This is hardly surprising since iron and steamship building was a very new industry. Consequently we can find examples like Charles Randolph whose father was a printer and stationer in Stirling; Joseph Russell's father was a cleric and a solicitor. William Tod Lithgow's father was a yarn merchant; among marine engineers, David Rowan's father was a slater, and J G Kincaid's father was a ship's captain.

Although such men had no previous family connection with shipbuilding, this does not mean they had no experience of the business when they attempted to set up their own companies. Shipbuilding was expanding so vigorously in the nineteenth century that there were many opportunities for individuals who gained experience in existing companies before setting up on their own. This was by far the most common route of entry for the men who were setting up business on Clydeside between the 1830s and the end of the century. A very large number of successful Clyde builders, as we have shown, trained with the Napiers. Charles Connell trained as an apprentice with Robert Steele of Greenock and then worked as yard manager for the Stephens in their Kelvinhaugh yard. William Tod Lithgow, who was partner to Joseph Russell, began in the drawing office of James Reid & Co in Port Glasgow; while Russell himself was apprenticed to J W Hoby & Co, engineers and shipbuilders in Renfrew.

This pattern of entry to the industry also gives the key to the training and skills of these successful men. With scant exception they came into shipbuilding through training as apprentices and then working as journeymen, foremen, and sometimes as managers in established shipyards and engine works. Their background was more as engineers and builders than as naval architects by their original training. Very few of these men had any theoretical or technical training before the last quarter of the nineteenth century. There were, of course, notable exceptions. William Pearce was Admiralty-trained at Chatham Dockyard, studying both as a naval architect and shipwright and coming to the Clyde first as a Lloyd's surveyor. Sir Thomas Bell, who rose to be managing director at John Brown's of Clydebank, began with J & G Thomson after qualifying at the Royal Naval Engineering College at Devonport.

The majority of the shipbuilders were therefore practical men whose skills grew and developed through experience on the job rather than from technical training. The stimulus of theory and book learning was injected into the system through the lively forum of the Institution of Engineers and Shipbuilders in Scotland, whose proceedings and transactions dating from 1857 indicate the thirst for knowledge, the wide scope of enquiry and problem solving, and the familiarity of the shipbuilders with the applied science as well as the craft of shipbuilding. Even so, few shipbuilders among the proprietors or senior partners were trained technical men, although there was some move in this direction toward the end of the century. Fred J Stephen took an MA at Glasgow University and attended the first classes in Naval Architecture under the new Elder Professor, Philip Jenkins. A little later Murray Stephen took a first class

QTSS *Aquitania* on sea trials in 1913. One of the giant transatlantic liners built by John Brown & Co. of Clydebank, and one of the first vessels to employ four steam turbines and quadruple screws. (By kind permission of University of Glasgow Archives)

honours in the Mechanical Science tripos at King's College, Cambridge, in 1914; in the same vein, Maurice Denny took a first class honours in Naval Architecture at the Massachusetts Institute of Technology in 1909. But in every case these men also followed a traditional apprenticeship either before or after their theoretical training. The Clydesiders believed in practical experience and in training on the job.

Since these men shared a common technical training with thousands of others in the industry, what was it that underlay their success? Was it purely family preferment or were there other factors? It is clear, for example, that some men established their personal reputation and the future success of their companies on the basis of invention and innovation. The Napiers, Robert, James and David, all had a significant role to play in developing the early steam engine and boilers. Charles Randolph and John Elder came together to give the industry the compound expansion engine and built their success upon that innovation. Similarly, Dr A C Kirk was the innovator of the triple expansion engine and it was that factor that led him to prominence as manager and ultimately controlling partner of Robert Napiers. While these were highly important developments, it is equally clear that most shipbuilding companies and most shipbuilders did not make their name on the basis of invention and innovation. For the vast majority the route to success lay in quick imitation, adaptation and improvement. James Gilchrist at Barclay Curle's was distinguished for improving the compound engines. Firms like the Stephens, the Inglis, D & W Henderson, J & G Thomson, and many others all built their reputation on sound and reliable construction. Their success was frequently linked to their establishing a name and reputation in a particular market specialism. Consequently, Joseph Russell and William Tod Lithgow led the Clyde in the building of semi-standardised cargo boats. Charles Connell adopted this pattern and he, too, achieved considerable success. The Dennys at Dumbarton had a notable name in the construction of river boats and ferries. The Stephens of Linthouse were distinguished builders of cargo liners, while a late incomer, Alfred Yarrow, made his name in torpedo boat destroyers.

The commercial skill of these men was in some ways even more important than their technical expertise. Building ships required sound commercial judgment and in some cases some of the Clyde builders carried this forward to astute investment in shipping. Peter Denny, William Lithgow, Charles Randolph, and Charles Connell were all significant investors in shipping lines and to a considerable extent their fortunes were more greatly enlarged there than in their shipyards. Somewhat more rarely there were, on occasion, individuals who built their success on sheer marketing flair. Perhaps the best example of this is Sir William Pearce. Pearce captured orders for his company by catching the popular imagination. Almost single handedly he devised the idea of the Blue Riband for vessels holding the record passage time on the North Atlantic. He set and established records for cross-Channel ferries and built his company's reputation on speed, style and safety. He was, in essence, a gambler; he took risks, he delivered, and succeeded.

Another notable characteristic of these men was their civic and philanthropic roles in their local communities. The Denny family made numerous contributions to their town of Dumbarton in the shape of schools, parks, housing, and in the establishment of three scholarships to Glasgow University. Similarly, the Lithgows were extensive patrons in Port Glasgow, notably of housing and the church. Charles Randolph gifted half his estate to the University of Glasgow; his partner's name is also remembered in the Elder Chair of Naval Architecture. In Govan, Elder is remembered through his wife's munificence in establishing Elder Park; the Elder Hospital commemorates his father. Most of the leading shipbuilders were active churchmen, and most served their local communities as Justices of the Peace, or as members of various boards on hospitals and schools. Local politics also occasionally attracted their service. James Gilchrist, for example, had involvement in all of these areas: he was Provost of Cove and Kilcreggan, an elder in Kilcreggan United Free Church, a founder of the St Andrew's Ambulance Association, a Justice of the Peace, a Deputy Lieutenant of the County and City of Glasgow, together with many other offices. His spread of civic and community involvement was not unusual among the shipbuilders. They were, however, primarily men with interests in their local areas. None of the major shipbuilders entered parliament, though most were active in the local branches of the Unionist and Liberal associations.

These successful men led busy and multi-faceted lives. For most the route to the top lay in family preferment, and it is clear that few of the leaders of the great firms were in themselves exceptional men in a technical sense. But they and their families did emerge from a whirling world of technical change, commercial insecurity, and vigorous competition. They succeeded where many more failed. Their dynasties did not grow by accident; they were built upon hard-headed business practice, autocratic paternalism in relation to the workforce and vigorous individualism in the pursuit of business. These were the characteristics of the shipbuilders who piloted their industry to world leadership in the course of the nineteenth century and created the legend 'Clyde built'.

Clydeside shipbuilders brought wealth and success to a number of families. Sir William Burrell sold the family shipping firm in 1917 to pursue his enthusiasm for collecting Medieval, Renaissance and Oriental art. These tangible results of Clydeside success can be seen now at the Burrell Collection in Glasgow.
Others developed an interest in less familiar cultures through working overseas. Among them was Major-General Robert Murdoch Smith who, after a distinguished career as engineer and expert in Persian art, became third Director of the Edinburgh Museum of Science and Art.

PERSIAN ART THROUGH THE EYES OF MAJOR-GENERAL ROBERT MURDOCH SMITH KCMG

Jennifer Scarce

The career of Robert-Murdoch Smith was characterised by a determination, energy and versatility which found an ideal outlet in his contribution to Persian art, a subject which was little known and understood in Europe during the nineteenth century.

Murdoch Smith was born at Bank Street, Kilmarnock on 18th August 1835, the second son of Hugh Smith, a medical practitioner, and his wife Jean Murdoch, who came of farming stock. This modest but secure family background ensured him a sound education at Kilmarnock Academy, where he was thoroughly instructed in the Greek and Latin classics, and at Glasgow University. Here he combined classical studies with courses in chemistry, moral and natural philosophy. Significantly for his future career, he took extracurricular studies in modern languages, achieving fluency in French and German and acquiring a working knowledge of Italian and some acquaintance with Arabic.

On graduation a promising opportunity arose when the army held the first open competition for commissions in the Ordnance Corps in 1855. Murdoch Smith came first out of 380 candidates in the qualifying examination and was gazetted to a lieutenant's commission on 24th September 1855, which he took up at the Royal Engineers' establishment at Chatham on 15th October. He had made a good beginning to an officer's career, but opportunities intervened which were to take full advantage of his resourceful nature and interesting qualifications. Charles Newton, later to become Keeper of Greek and Roman Antiquities in the British Museum, was investigating the remains of classical Halicarnassus near the Turkish port of Bodrum and, requiring some technical personnel, requested an officer and four sappers of the Royal Engineers. Murdoch Smith was chosen and spent the years 1856-9 assisting with the excavation of the famous tomb of Mausolus of 4th century BC date, on which he submitted a detailed technical report. This experience, which stimulated an appetite for archaeological and historical research, was followed from 1860 to 1861 by excavations at Cyrene, an important Graeco-Roman city site in Libya, which he undertook on his own initiative.

Understandably these experiences outside the scope of a normal military career encouraged Murdoch Smith to seek other opportunities. These arose when a Telegraph Convention was signed in 1863 between Britain and Persia for the construction of a land telegraph system linking London with India. Murdoch Smith answered an advertisement in *The Times* for Royal Engineers officers to supervise the work, and in 1864 arrived in Persia to take up a post as superintendent of the Tehran-Kohrud section of the line. His success was remarkable, as in 1865 he was appointed Director of the Persian Telegraph Department with the local rank of Major. His work was varied and demanding, involving supervision of the

Portrait of Sir Robert Murdoch Smith. A polychrome underglaze tile made by Ali Mahommed Isfahani and dated 1304 H (1887 AD).(NMS)

administration and accounts of the Persian Telegraph Department and long journeys around Persia inspecting the telegraph line and stations. The surviving volumes of his correspondence covering the years 1867 to 1887 are revealing of his own attitudes to Persia, which were perceptive and sympathetic, and of the problems of a country caught between a traditional way of life and the entry of western technology. He was well regarded by the Persians especially as he learned their language and was soon immersed in their considerable artistic achievements. This admiration for Persian art was to develop into a tangible project, namely the building up of a comprehensive collection for the South Kensington Museum (now the Victoria and Albert Museum).

He contacted the Museum during the only long period of home leave, from 1871 to 1873, of his Persian career, offering his services as a roving agent reporting on objects of Persian art suitable for purchase. His knowledge of the Persian language and people, his network of local telegraph officials and his regular journeys throughout Persia, plus his enthusiasm and energy gave him exceptional advantages, and the Museum sensibly accepted his offer. He

Sir Robert Murdoch
Smith, c1885, the source
of the portrait on the
tile. (NMS)

wasted no time, as is seen in a letter of 3rd November 1873, where he reports his first acquisitions.

> I have the honour to report that I have already purchased a considerable collection of old Persian fayence, a suit of damascened steel consisting of helmet, armpiece and shield, a number of carved metal vessels of different kinds and a few other articles of artistic interest. As the articles are upwards of 80 in number I must reserve a detailed report regarding them for the next mail to England, as this one leaves almost immediately.
>
> I hope to take the opportunity of an official tour of inspection in the beginning of 1874 to carry the articles above referred to (and any others I may purchase in the meantime) with me to Bushire, whence they can be shipped direct to London via the Suez Canal, thereby — avoiding the numerous trans-shipments and long land journeys by the Caspian on the Black Sea.

To this letter he appended the first of the 68 reports he was to submit to the South Kensington Museum between 1873 and 1885, which are a fascinating record of collecting. They show how he was at pains to be systematic, how he came to sensible financial arrangements with the Museum, and how he tackled transport problems.

One of his most spectacular achievements was the acquisition of the collection of a certain Monsieur Jules Richard who had first come to Persia around 1844-6 and had taught French at Tehran's technical college — the Dar al-Funun. Murdoch Smith reported to the South Kensington Museum in 1875.

I have recently examined in a cursory manner a very valuable collection of Persian artistic articles belonging to M Richard a French Mussulman who has long been resident in Tehran. The Collection comprises articles of almost every class and has been formed gradually in the course of nearly 30 years. Most of the objects are packed away in boxes but I am now getting them unpacked and a catalogue made. I have induced M Richard to agree to my proposal to fix a price for each article at such prices to give the Museum the refusal of the whole or any portion of the collection.

As a further inducement he added that 'Many of the articles now belonging to M Richard are now not to be found elsewhere'.

The Museum agreed that Murdoch Smith should purchase the Richard collection on its behalf. The objects were packed in 62 boxes and conveyed to Bushire for shipment to London, accompanied by a warrant from a high-ranking Persian official, the Sepahsalar Azem, exempting it from all customs duty. News of its safe arrival was appropriately telegraphed to Murdoch Smith in December 1875.

True to its educational role the Museum was not content with the acquisition of the objects alone, and requested Murdoch Smith to write a handbook to accompany a large-scale exhibition. This introduced Persian art to the British public and established Murdoch Smith's reputation as a pioneer scholar in the field. The exhibition, which opened in April 1876, displayed 3517 objects divided between categories of metalwork, arms and armour, enamels on metal, goldsmith's and silversmith's work, carvings in stone, manuscripts, book covers, paintings, woodwork and papier-maché, musical instruments, embroidery and needlework, pottery, tiles, glass, and ranging in date from the twelfth to nineteenth centuries. Reactions to the exhibition varied from public amazement at the exotic and colourful splendour of Persian art to thoughtful and painstaking reviews in such newspapers as the *Times, Atheneum, Daily News,* and *Morning Post.* In particular the *Daily News* added 'the pleasure of the visitor is much enhanced by a very excellent handbook, written in Persia by Major R Murdoch Smith RE, a welcome addition to that admirable series of cheap art handbooks of which Mr Cunliffe Owen, the director of South Kensington Museum, is justly proud'.

The catalogue accompanying an exhibition is indispensable both as a record and as a serious contribution to the subject. Murdoch Smith's handbook in a lucid account of facts and theories of Persian art currently available to him and tempered by his own field observations concerning technique and function. It remains an essential source for the artifacts of the late eighteenth to nineteenth century period, notably textiles and metalwork, which as yet are still insufficiently researched.

The success of the 1876 exhibition was followed by other projects. Murdoch Smith continued to work with M Richard and began to enlist the services of his Telegraph employees, such as Sydney Churchill.

He also succeeded in interesting eminent Persians in the South Kensington Museum, notably Nasiruddin Shah (who ruled Persia from 1848 to 1896) who through one of his ministers donated a valuable gift in 1877 which was recorded by Murdoch Smith.

H.E., the Emin al Mulk, has sent me an assortment of 14 carpets and pieces of Resht embroidery and that he is now in search of specimens of other fabrics so as to make H.M.'s present a collec-

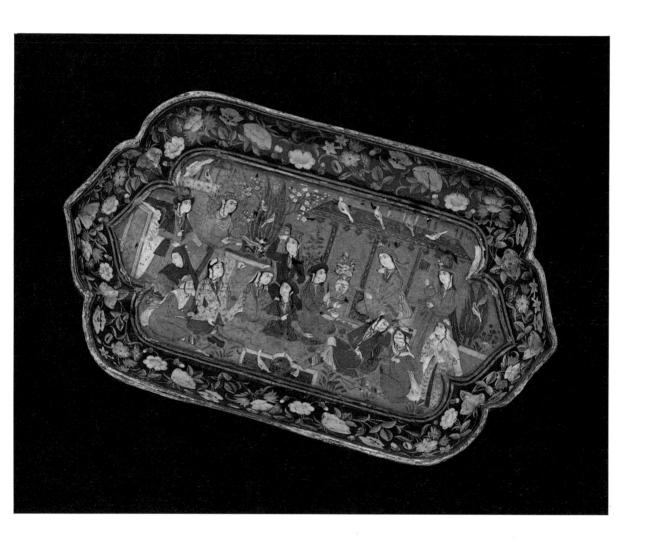

Painted and varnished
papier-mache 'lacquer'
tray acquired by the
Edinburgh Museum of
Science and Art during
Murdoch Smith's
directorship. The
picture illustrates a 15th
century Persian poem,
'Yussuf and Zulaikha',
by the famous poet
Jami. (NMS)

The fossil fish, *osteolepis,* from Tynet Burn, Banffshire, acquired by Hugh Miller and part of the collection which came to the Industrial Museum of Scotland in 1859. (NMS)

tion of all the principal textiles in Persia. In choosing one class of objects, and that textiles, for presentation, H.M. is following the suggestion I made last year to the Emin al Mulk as reported in my letters No 28 of May 22nd and No 29 of June 16th 1876. My reasons for making the suggestion were first the idea of a present of modern textiles would probably commend itself to H.M.'s mind as an indirect means of increasing the trade of his own country; and 2ndly that whatever sum H.M. might devote to the purpose would be better expended on one class of objects than if it were frittered away on many.

Nasiruddin Shah's gift of fine carpets and embroideries may be seen in the Museum today and is revealing of both his taste and Murdoch Smith's farsighted awareness that a sequence of contemporary documented material is the foundation of future research.

Murdoch Smith's involvement with Persian art neither stopped with the South Kensington Museum nor with his retirement from active Persian service in 1885, when he was presented with a Sword of Honour by Nasiruddin Shah in recognition of his work. He was appointed Director of the Edinburgh Museum of Science and Art (now the Royal Museum of Scotland) in 1885, a post which he held until his death in 1900. He did visit Persia once more in 1887 on telegraph and diplomatic business. On this occasion the least complicated of his tasks was the presentation of gifts from Queen Victoria to Nasiruddin Shah and other members of the Persian royal family, which included 'a set of instruments for a military band of sixty men, especially made by Boosey and Co, of London and finished in the highest style of their art'. Nasiruddin Shah enjoyed military music and showed his appreciation of the gift by presenting Murdoch Smith with a diamond encrusted gold snuff box.

Murdoch Smith finally retired from the Persian Telegraph Department and the army on 13th December 1887 with the honorary rank of Major-General and the award of a Knight Commander of the Order of St Michael and St George (KCMG) in the New Year Honours List of 1888. Henceforth he concentrated on his work at the Edinburgh Museum of Science and Art, where his most enduring achievement was the development of the collections of Persian art. He made the most of his still active contacts with Telegraph staff in Persia to acquire a good and representative collection of material. The Museum records and correspondence during his Directorship provide evidence of purchases made through Sydney Churchill, Preece, Ernst Hoeltzer, and John Fahie, who were all employed as station superintendants. Notable examples include fine metalwork acquired in 1886 through Sydney Churchill, two outstanding pieces of thirteenth century lustre-painted tilework, bought in 1888 and 1891, and a large collection of textiles from Ernst Hoeltzer in 1888. He was again in contact with M Richard, who was concerned to dispose of the remaining items of his collection, and negotiated to obtain shares of the collection for both the Edinburgh and South Kensington Museums. The Edinburgh Museum's share included armour, weapons, glass, ceramics, lacquer and textiles of the seventeenth to the nineteenth centuries. Murdoch Smith organised an exhibition of the Persian material and wrote a short guidebook to provide supplementary information.

During his years in Edinburgh he was able to develop his interests in contemporary Persian crafts with special reference to ceramic tilework. He had already realised during his collecting activities for the South Kensington Museum the importance of such material, as he had included some modern examples. In Edinburgh he exhibited some examples as noted in the guide, 'A mantlepiece and a number of tiles by Ali Mahommed, a potter of the present day, are well worthy of notice'. Further investigations into his correspondence and the museum records reveal that he had built up a relationship with this potter, who had worked both in Isfahan and Tehran during the 1870s and 1880s, and had constantly encouraged him in his career. He eventually persuaded him to write an account of his craft methods 'On the Manufacture of Modern Kashi Earthenware Tiles and Vases' as noted in a letter of 1888.

> I have the honour to inform you that I have this day sent by parcel post to your address a package containing the specimens of Persian pigments which you were good enough to forward to me some time ago. I have taken a small portion of each for this Museum. With each specimen I have wrapped up a translation of the Persian label inscribed on its cover. The package also contains a few sheets of printed labels (translated) and ten copies (translated into English by Mr Fargues of the Telegraph Department Teheran) of the account of his process of enamelled tile making written at my request by Ustad Ali Mahommed of Teheran.

This account was published in Edinburgh in 1888.

The relationship between Ali Mahommed and Murdoch Smith is perhaps most charmingly summed up in the set of portrait tiles which the potter made in 1887. They are flamboyant creations worked in a fluent underglaze polychrome technique in which traditional Persian motifs of palmettes, scrolling foliage and roses frame an oval portrait medallion of Murdoch Smith treated in a subtle hatched manner in sepia tones influenced by contemporary photographs. A Persian inscription 'Portrait of Colonel Robert Murdoch Esmit, honoured gentleman 1304 (1887 AD)' leaves no room for doubt. An appropriate epilogue for Robert Murdoch Smith's career was the reception given for Nasiruddin Shah during his third visit to Europe, which was held in the Edinburgh Museum of Science and Art on 23rd July 1889.

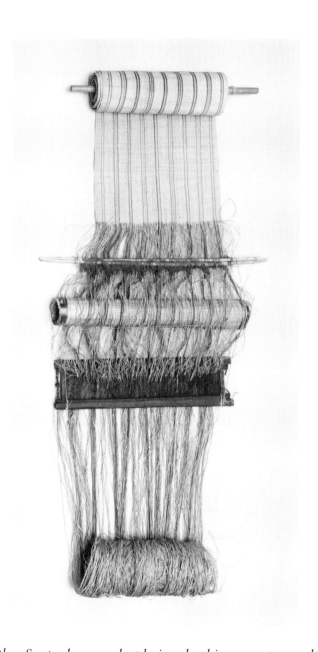

*Another Scot who was deeply involved in an eastern culture
was Dr Neil Gordon Munro, who spent many years in Japan,
where he became Director of the Yokohama General Hospital.
Between 1908 and 1914 he collected archaeological
specimens, Ainu ethnographical material and some
contemporary Japanese arts and crafts. The Ainu backstrap
loom above, used for weaving the inner bark of elm, is
amongst the material he gave to the Royal Scottish Museum.
Contributions from those who remained at home were also
important. Sir Joseph Noel Paton lived and worked mainly in
Scotland, and was not only a collector, but a notable and
popular painter.*

SIR JOSEPH NOEL PATON

Hugh Cheape

The name of Noel Paton bulks large in the history of art in Scotland in the second half of the nineteenth century. He was the most prominent figure of a small group of artists who achieved remarkable popularity in their day, his paintings possessing charm as well as power, both qualities which appealed to the contemporary mind.

It can be said, without a hint of irony, that Sir Joseph Noel Paton was a worthy. Though true 'worthies' can only be appreciated in retrospect, he made a strong impression on his contemporaries in the high Victorian era. When he died in December 1901, *The Times* obituarist commented that: 'His pictures seem curiously old-fashioned to modern eyes', and added as though to compensate for this harsh subjective judgement, '. . . through all his life, he was animated by high aims and noble impulses'. These are both recurring notes among Noel Paton's younger contemporaries at the close of the nineteenth century. A serious and dignified *persona* was generally deeply respected and it was this quality in Noel Paton that made him a worthy and laid the foundation of his reputation in his own community of Edinburgh and among his fellow countrymen.

Students of the long standing debate in psychology on the respective influences of congenital inheritance and of nurture and upbringing would find it difficult to separate these strands in Noel Paton's make-up. He was born in Dunfermline on 13th December 1821 in the prosaically named Wooers' Alley in the old grey town of loom shops, and brought up there. Dunfermline was the capital of the linen damask trade and in the nineteenth century one of the last retreats of commercial handloom weaving. The Paton's spacious and pleasant villa in Wooers' Alley was sufficient testimony to the family's material success. Their modest prosperity was recent, due largely to Joseph Neil Paton's career as a leading textile designer in one of the linen damask mills. He had probably inherited little from his own father except no doubt for a strain of enterprise and artistry. It was said that Noel Paton's grandfather, David Paton, had collected old Ballads and stories 'being all that his purse allowed'. He had however put together a printing press about 1810 and had made the type with which he printed ballads and religious controversies and his own rhyming history of Dunfermline.

Joseph Neil Paton in his maturity had a secure local reputation as an artist-designer and the respective successes of his children must bear witness to his skill and ability. Joseph Noel was of course knighted for his contribution to art. His brother Waller Hugh Paton was a fine landscape painter whose work may be said to have stood the test of time more successfully than Sir Noel's. Their sister Amelia, who later married the painter and pioneer photographer David Octavius Hill, was known in her own right as a sculptress.

Sir Joseph Noel Paton
painted by John
Ballantyne. (National
Galleries of Scotland)

Noel Paton's father's work allowed him the novel luxury of leisure. He was a Fellow of the Society of Antiquaries of Scotland and a collector, and decorated the house in Wooers' Alley with his collection of casts, *objets d'art* and engravings after the appropriate old masters, all in the best traditions of the Renaissance as the inspiration to the craft of collecting. He reserved the warmth and pleasure of sentiment for Scottish antiquities, the term usually applied to an almost random collection of prehistoric artifacts, historical and ethnological material, relics of memorable, famous and notorious events and persons; such was the enthusiasm of this sort of collecting urge that the most spurious, imaginary and even false associations would be accepted as qualifying a piece for a collection of antiquities. Joseph Paton's collection was not altogether free of this stigma. To dwell on this would be niggardly when we see that the father's enthusiasm fired the son and that his love of local history preserved many interesting relics when the hand of progress was making a clean sweep of the old town.

After school in Dunfermline, the young Noel Paton was apprenticed as a draughtsman-designer in the textile industry, in Paisley, which had made its name in the second half of the eighteenth century with the manufacture of fine linen fabrics. He entered the successful local muslin weaving industry and the demands of accuracy, finesse and detail, central both in the design and manufacture of this fabric, must surely have helped to create these same standards in the young artist that were the distinctive hallmark of so much of his later artistic work.

His paintings, which entailed massive research and study in their preparation, always contained a welter of detail, the minutest element of which was fully elaborated. A criticism of his composition often levelled at Noel Paton was that the overall balance of a picture suffered at the expense of this detail. Intense observation and attention to detail were however central to Noel Paton's work and this places him firmly in the ranks of the nineteenth century romantics. It arose out of the desire to see the past, in the words of the German historian Ranke, 'as it really was', and was also inspired by Scott's portrayal of the manners and morals of ages past. Both historians and painters worked over their ground with scrupulous care, their methodologies being the fruits of the new discipline of history.

In 1843, Noel Paton gained a studentship in the London Academy Schools and it was there that he met John Millais and formed a lifelong friendship with him. The Pre-Raphaelite Brotherhood was not formally founded until 1848 and perhaps had Noel Paton remained in London, he would have become a member, given that he clearly sympathised with their aims and was working in a style which was similar in outlook. His possibly premature return from London to Scotland in 1844 cut short his formal artistic training and may account for obvious shortcomings in his work, such as the often uneven treatment of vivid colouring. Other nineteenth century Scottish painters who went south and continued to work in London, seem to have remained subsequently more in the public eye.

The ten years or so after his return from London were extremely fruitful and helped to establish his reputation. In 1844 and 1845, he exhibited his first paintings at the Royal Scottish Academy, *Ruth Gleaning, Rachel weeping for her Children* and *The Holy Family*, clearly demonstrating his liking for Gospel scenes. This might suggest that his art was limited, when in fact he swam freely in other popular artistic nineteenth century currents while remaining constant to what can now be seen as the acceptable range of themes and subjects. These were regulated by the Academies and by the conservative reaction of traditional patronage in royalty and the aristocracy and also in the ranks of new wealth. Official art remained secure until criticism came out into the open towards the close of the nineteenth century. There were powerful reasons for official art becoming so firmly established, and the Westminster Hall Competitions in which Noel Paton was successful are an example.

On the memorable night of 16th October 1834, fire swept through the Houses of Parliament. The sense of national disaster and relentless destruction was caught by Turner in his famous painting of the event. The rebuilding of the Palace of Westminster was planned rapidly and executed slowly. A competition for the design produced the fertile combination of Barry with Pugin, the latter producing his tour de force of the Gothic style before his premature death in 1852. The refurbishment of the Houses of Parliament with painting and sculpture owed more than a little to the pervasive influence of the new Prince Consort's earnest belief in the elevating qualities of art. A series of competitions was held beginning in 1843 for cartoons for monumental frescoes and drew vast historical and allegorical can-

'Reconciliation of Oberon and Titania' by Sir Joseph Noel Paton, one of his most admired paintings. (National Galleries of Scotland)

vasses from mural painters, several of whom made instant reputations and even considerable fortunes.

Noel Paton sent a fresco, *The Spirit of Religion,* to the Westminster Hall Competitions in 1845 and was awarded a prize. As much as any of his work, this painting with its careful allegorical formula symbolises his preference for the spiritual rather than the historical-religious or straightforward Gospel subject-matter. In 1847, he sent another two paintings, *Christ bearing the Cross* and his celebrated and intricately detailed *Reconciliation of Oberon and Titania* and again was rewarded; this last painting was the subject of considerable admiration and comment, and there was keen competition to acquire it. 'The King of the Belgians, it was said, had resolved to become its owner', as a contemporary observed. The artist painted several other pictures in 1847 in which Oberon and Titania were the central characters in scenes taken from *A Midsummer Night's Dream.* He was the only Scottish painter of his generation to make extensive use of the nude figure in his paintings, and his treatment of the figure of Oberon and Titania can hardly be said to be mystical. Around and behind the lush central figures, the fairies abound in erotic detail, the propriety of which would have been called into question were it not for the licence of midsummer madness and enchantment.

Noel Paton followed the fairy theme in 1849 in his *Quarrel of Oberon and Titania.* These paintings were so popular when they were exhibited because fairies were in vogue by the nineteenth century. They were enjoying a respectability outwith the credulity of folk belief to which they had been banished by humanist learning in the sixteenth century. The nineteenth century version was far removed from the realms of horror and the powers of evil, although the revival of taste for the Gothic yearned for a frisson from encounters with the supernatural.

Noel Paton's distinction in the Westminster Hall Competitions had come early and success at the age of twenty-four was a matter for congratulation. In the 1860s a notable series of paintings based on Arthurian legend produced *Lancelot of the Lake, Sir Galahad and the Angel, The Barge of King Arthur,* and *Sir Galahad and the Vision of the Holy Grail.* The community and ideals of Arthur's court survived so tenaciously in English due to Sir Thomas Malory's translations published by Caxton in 1485 and their frequent republications in the course of the nineteenth century. The appeal of Arthurian romance to the Victorian mind is highlighted above all by the success of Alfred Lord Tennyson whose 'Idylls of the King', of Arthur, his knights and the noble design of the Round Table, were published in 1859. The essence of Noel Paton's Arthurian paintings lies in the symbolical treatment of the central characters and the infusion in them of an element of his own upbringing in the literature of Scottish history, drawing on Barbour's 'Bruce', Blind Hary's 'Wallace', Macpherson's 'Ossian' and the Border Minstrelsy. Arthur becomes, *more Scotico,* the undying hero of the north and the promised deliverer. Apart from the spiritual content, his Arthurian pictures are vehicles for the results of acute observation, research and his own strong penchant for collecting.

One of Noel Paton's delightful legacies is his own *Catalogue* of his collection of arms, armour and antiquities, subsequently acquired by the Royal Scottish Museum in 1905, 'His collection was his only hobby', a younger contemporary remarked. It was privately printed in Edinburgh in 1879 in a limited edition of two hundred copies, embellished on the title page with his own arms and motto 'Do richt and fear nocht', and three small vignettes of a seal matrix, a pilgrim's badge and a decorated sword pommel. The *Private Catalogue* is prefaced by a wistful memorial and a modest disclaimer:

> This Catalogue is designed only for my family and for those friends who may be supposed likely to feel some interest in objects from which I have derived much unalloyed pleasure and many of which are endeared to me by early associations. In its arrangement no classification has been attempted. My purpose has rather been, by recording the existing collocation of the respective objects, to preserve some impression of the internal aspect of a house of which I would fain hope some kindly memories may survive when its present occupant is gone where there is reason to apprehend Old Iron is not.

For visitors to the artist's home at 33 George Square in the 1870s and 1880s, the *Catalogue* would have formed a logical accompaniment to their progress round the house, with its seven sections moving from barbican to donjon, from gatehouse to inner sanctum.

Noel Paton was by any standards an interesting man, cultured and widely read. This is borne out by a series of learned, even piquant papers in the *Proceedings* of the Society of Antiquaries of Scotland of which he was a Fellow. When describing the Battle Abbey Sword in a piece in 1872, he chastised the government for failing to buy one of the great arms collections then being broken up. 'Such events' he said with a note of stern reprimand, 'happen but rarely in the history of civilised nations and are not soon forgotten . . . so much for imperial cheese-paring.' The results of the trophies of arms which Noel Paton created can be seen in his densely packed illustrations for W E

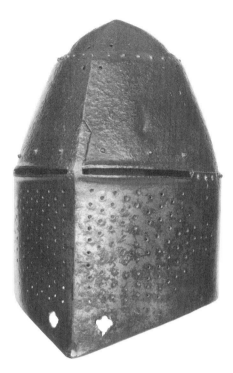

14th century helm belonging to Sir Richard Pembridge, a leading captain in Edward III's wars against the French. This was one of the most important items in Noel Paton's collection of arms and armour acquired by the Royal Scottish Museum in 1905. (NMS)

Aytoun's *Lays of the Scottish Cavaliers* published by Blackwood in 1863. No detail of weaponry or accoutrements is ignored or neglected. No social detail is unexploited although the bias of the artist and his age stands out starkly.

Controversy over religious issues ancient and modern lies at the heart of recent Scottish history and indeed helps to throw light on Noel Paton's approach to art. The religious loyalties and affiliations of Noel Paton's father were unusual even among dissenting Scots, but perhaps not surprising in one bred among the weavers, notorious for their sturdy radicalism, religious casuistry and determined independence. Certainly Joseph Neil Paton's religious beliefs impressed themselves on his contemporaries as much as his collection of art and antiquities. Evangelicalism in the Scottish church had tended to absorb itself in the long running battle over patronage and church government, and secession from the establishment when it came was a cathartic revolution to perpetuate the true church and congregational rights in the face of falsehood and treachery, harking back to the religious strife of the seventeenth century covenants.

The creation of the Relief Church by Rev Thomas Gillespie near Dunfermline itself in 1752 was a notable introduction of independency and dissent, the liberalism of which gave vent to debate and schism. This coincided with the arrival of Methodism in Scotland. The radical stream in Scottish theology flourished until the witch hunts against political radicalism in the early 1790s.

Noel Paton's grandfather was a Unitarian, an extreme dissenter even by the standards of the home of the Relief Church. His father was successively a Methodist, a Quaker and a Swedenborgian. These strands in Noel Paton's background have been the subject of passing comment by biographers and obituarists but they have not been subjected to the analysis which they deserve. Noel Paton himself was partly educated as a Quaker and although he dutifully attended the

Kirk he seemed to have remained unorthodox in his views and quietly critical of the establishment. It would be surprising if his antecedent dissenting and non-conformist family traditions did not colour his art as well as his thought. In fact, his paintings, so many of which were religious, amount to very telling documents and suggest that his art was deeply affected by unresolved tensions within his own character arising from two generations or more of non-conformity.

Noel Paton was elected an Academician in 1850 and became one of Queen Victoria's favourite painters. She appointed him Her Majesty's Limner in 1866 and he was knighted in 1867. The University of Edinburgh honoured him with an Honorary Doctorate in 1876 and Dunfermline with the Freedom of the Burgh in 1881. Public recognition and reward however may not have counted for much beside his happy marriage to Margaret Ferrier and their prodigious family of ten children.

Noel Paton's success and inventiveness is generally considered to have declined about 1870, perhaps not surprising after around thirty years of sustained effort. For the next decade, he concentrated on religious themes, one or two paintings standing out such as his *Faith and Reason* and *Christ and Mary at the Sepulchre*. Others produced in this period of his life contributed considerably to his reputation.

His name became familiar through engravings of a group of his religious paintings *Faith and Reason, Dawn* or *Luther at Erfurt, The Man of Sorrows,* and *Christ the Good Shepherd.* His painting *The Pursuit of Pleasure* serves as an example of how business was conducted in the new nineteenth century world of the art dealer. The work was exhibited at the Royal Scottish Academy which of course brought it to public notice. An Edinburgh printer bought it from him for £1,000, had it engraved, sold the prints widely and resold the painting itself for 2,000 guineas. The business was speculative and competitive but profits were always expected. Noel Paton benefited also from another ploy which popularised works of art. They were toured around the country and exhibited under lights in lectures to an enthusiastic public. His *Lux in Tenebris* of 1879 is an example of this, the lecture in this case amounting to a sermon.

From the standpoint of the twentieth century, at least until recently, Scottish artists of the Victorian era have not been well served, victims only perhaps of the ruthless see-saw of taste and fashion rather than deserving of a blanket disregard. Many of them seem to have suffered from the same critical stigma as implied in the term 'kailyard' which has attached itself to nineteenth century Scottish works of fiction. Social and domestic scenes lovingly and sentimentally drawn in prose certainly had their counterparts on canvas.

The other significant theme in Victorian art was religion presented in such a way as to impart a moral message. Noel Paton concentrated on the whole on serious paintings with symbolic content, appearing to give himself up most completely to the allegory of his religious pictures, hence the undeniable popularity of the trio *The Man with the Muckrake, The Choice* and *Mors Janua Vitae.* Given the general currents of fashion for religious subjects among nineteenth century painters, the quality of intensity in Noel Paton's treatment of this subject matter was very personal. This intensity, seen in the wider context of eighteenth and nineteenth century history, is a clue to the importance and popularity of an art that responded to the needs and tastes of the times.

Sir Joseph Noel Paton interpreted religious subjects for a responsive Victorian audience. Beyond Victorian Scotland missionaries carried a more austere Christian message to peoples of very different backgrounds. The Bible woman of Siao Chang (above) gave Bible readings and her husband preached. The family was evangelised by the Rev J D Liddell, Congregationalist missionary and father of Eric Liddell, the runner. In 1898 J D Liddell went initially to Mongolia, but two years later was forced to flee the Boxer Rebellion. Scottish missionary and educational activity was important in other parts of the East, especially in India. Dr Andrew Bell was an educator who applied the lessons of his experiences in India to educational reform in Britain.

ANDREW BELL: AN EXPERIMENT IN INDIA

Jenni Calder

In June 1787 the son of a St Andrews barber arrived in the southern Indian city of Madras. He was 34 years old and had already had an unusually diverse career which reflected an aptitude not only for enterprise but for opportunism. His name, Andrew Bell, has since the end of the eighteenth century been associated with education in Scotland, England and abroad.

Bell's background was also enterprising, although his mother, from a family of modest achievers in the professions, succumbed to insanity. His father was a barber of distinction, known in St Andrews as an artist, a wig-maker who 'built up enormous edifices of horse-hair, grease and flour, without which no professor could lecture and no judge could try a case'. He was on familiar terms with the St Andrews intelligentsia, and his interest in practical mathematics and natural philosophy, or physics, was inherited by his son.

A powerful influence in Andrew Bell's career in education was clearly his own unhappiness at school. Whatever the virtues of the Scottish education system and its encouragement of the under-privileged, this was a time of rigidity and authoritarianism in schooling. Bell himself said, 'I never went to a school without trembling. I could not tell whether I should be flogged or not'. He was happier at St Andrews University, through which he paid his way by teaching, and achieved considerable distinction as a student. But there seemed few opportunities in Scotland for an acute and ambitious young man, and in 1774 he left for Virginia, at a time when the American colonies were boiling up for their revolt from British government.

Little is known about how Bell spent his first years in Virginia, or how he reacted to the political and military turmoil around him. But in 1779 he became tutor to a planter family called Braxton, and seems to have been a great success, not only in his educational duties but in the tobacco dealing in which he was also involved. When in 1781 he left Yorktown to return to Scotland, there was a large sum owing him for tobacco he had sold. Most of the money he would never see, for events in the colonies devastated the tobacco trade.

By the time Bell returned to Scotland, both his interest in education and his driving ambition were apparent. So was his quixotry. Back in St Andrews he fought a duel, and in his extreme short-sightedness fired indiscriminately at the seconds, fortunately without fatal consequence. He was soon on the move again, and in September 1784 was ordained in the Church of England. This was not the only unexpected turn in Bell's career.

He returned to Scotland to become chaplain to the Episcopal Chapel at Leith, and although he did not linger there Leith would become a beneficiary of Bell's later success. His modest role at Leith was too limiting, and he began to look further afield. Like many other Scots in need of occupation he set his sights on India.

In the last quarter of the eighteenth century the East India Company was consolidating and expanding its position in India. The French had been defeated, and the internal dissensions of the Indian states opened the way for increasing British intrusion and a stronger British presence. To protect the interests of the East India Company and the many personnel involved in spreading the network of trade and administration an army was required. It was this army that under Clive and then Wellesley defeated the French and successive resistant Indian princes.

Dr Andrew Bell, educational reformer and publicist. (National Galleries of Scotland)

The Company operated from London, but there was a strong Scottish involvement, which helped many Scots to openings either with the Company or in aspects of the India trade connected with it. There were also, in the last decades of the eighteenth century, increasing attempts to break the EIC's monopoly, and in these Scots also played a prominent role. Bell may not have been directly involved in commercial activities in India, but he certainly benefited from the accessible wealth, and returned from Madras with a substantial fortune. He even made money during the voyage to Madras by running classes for the officers on board.

In Madras Bell was offered the job of superintendent of the Military Male Asylum which was being set up at Egmore Redoubt, a deserted fort just outside the city. He also found himself with several other appointments, mainly chaplaincies to a number of British regiments. The Asylum was set up by the EIC to educate the 'orphan' sons of British soldiers (priority given to the offspring of officers) and Indian mothers. The boys were discouraged from maintaining contact with their 'maternal relatives'. It was an interesting exercise in colonial responsibility, but at first it seemed as if it would be an exercise without tangible results. Bell was, as his biographer Robert Southey put it, 'dissatisfied with the want of discipline, and the imperfect instruction in every part of the school'. Southey provides a clue as to Bell's personality and methods when he adds, 'Dr Bell's temper led him to do all things quickly, and his habit of mind to do them thoroughly, and leave nothing incomplete'.

Bell, who declined a salary for this job, set about transforming both principle and practice in education at the Madras Asylum, and having done that devoted the rest of his life to carrying out the same task in Britain and further afield. He devised what became known as the 'Madras System', using monitors and pupil teachers, with the further advanced pupils teaching those a step or two behind. Bell called it 'mutual tuition', and aimed for a situation in which a single supervising teacher could run an entire school.

The Asylum's teachers resisted, but Bell's system worked, initiated by a bright eleven year old who became his first pupil teacher. Before long Bell was able to claim 'I think I have made great progress in a very difficult attempt, and almost wrought a complete change in the morals and character of a generation of boys'. In spite of his own harsh experience Bell retained a committed belief in discipline but, although he was impatient and of a 'combustible disposition' he established a real rapport with his pupils. His success at Madras was due partly to this, but it also owed a great deal to Bell's love not only of teaching but of management.

One of Bell's pupils was William Smith, in whom there was such confidence that at the age of 17 he accompanied an embassy to Tippoo Sultan, in order to conduct 'a course of experiments in natural philosophy' for the Sultan's benefit. The Madras government sent to Tippoo 'an extensive and elegant philosophical and mathematical apparatus' — what we know of Bell's interest in such things suggests that he made the selection — as a present, and it was William Smith's task to explain and demonstrate these.

Tippoo Sultan's enthusiasm for mechanical devices was well known: the famous Tippoo's Tiger, a mechanical beast in the act of devouring a Scottish gentleman now at the Victoria and Albert museum, illustrates this. He seems to have reacted keenly to Smith's experiments, as Smith himself reported in a letter to Bell in 1794.

. . . the following were exhibited: tumbler and balls, sealing wax, twelve shocked men, among whom were several khans and vacheels — electric stool; a man of eminent rank stood, and the Sultaun applied the hand about the man to receive shocks. Inflammable air fired; at which he was astonished at first, and afterwards greatly pleased.

Bell must have been delighted at this vindication of his method. But he apparently had no evangelical inclinations towards the Indians themselves, and one cannot help wondering what kind of future lay ahead of the Asylum's half-caste alumni in a colonial world which, whatever their education, was unlikely to accept them as British.

In 1796, his health suffering from the Madras climate, Bell returned to Britain, and from that time on his pre-eminent and obsessive concern was to introduce the 'Madras System' as widely as possible. The remainder of his career was active, dedicated and contentious. In 1797 he published *An Experiment in Education, made at the Male Asylum of Madras,* in which he argued for 'the opening up of a new epoch in the science of education, and of the application of the powers of the new engine [his system] to the improvement of youth, the amelioration of society, and the best interests of Church and State.'

His conviction in his method was unshakeable, and this combined with his obsessive and irascible nature generated some hostility. But his system, and the similar independently conceived approach of Joseph Lancaster, a very different personality — ostentatious, recklessly extravagant, but equally confident — was introduced in a number of schools. The two men were at first mutually supportive but, perhaps inevitably, their relationship disintegrated into embattled rivalry.

Bell's dedication to publicising his system did not cause him to neglect his career, which went from strength to strength, and by 1819 he was canon at Westminster Abbey. He travelled abroad, had influence with rulers and officials in Europe and America, and was highly respected. A man of considerable means, he bought and ran an estate near Castle Douglas in Galloway. On his death he left £200,000. A large part of this was used to set up schools in Leith, St Andrews, Cupar, Aberdeen and Edinburgh. It also helped to finance two chairs of education, at the universities of Edinburgh and St Andrews.

As a later biographer, J M D Meiklejohn, himself a professor of education, put it:

Andrew Bell was an extraordinary man. I may even go so far as to say he was an extraordinary Scotchman. In a country where every man has been framed in a mould, which was afterwards broken and no copy kept, it argued considerable force of mind or character to distinguish oneself at all.

A quirky individualist and a canny businessman, as well as an educational reformer of profound conviction and wide influence, Dr Andrew Bell's achievement lies not so much in his 'system' as in his drawing attention to educational needs and his constructive efforts towards supplying them. Characteristic of a career that was quixotic and unpredictable, the doctorate was an MD irrelevantly and illogically bestowed by St Andrews University before his departure to India.

152

	Bar.	Ther.	Wind	Rain.
	28·2	76	E	3·09
	28·05	80	SE	
	28·1	80	SE	

1876 Thursday

Mr Young, & Dr Laws both suffered severely from fever during the night, but were rather better in the morning.

On arriving at Mapondas, the banks were lined with crowds of people as usual. Sam & Joe were sent ashore in the boat to enquire if Maponda could be seen & to bring Mrs Wakotani off in the boat. They soon returned bringing W. & telling us Sam had seen Maponda, who would be delighted to receive a visit from us.

Wakotani informed us that the boys had slept at Maponda's village, the 4th or 5th night after leaving C. Maclear. that they had not asked W. to go with them, that they had not got a canoe at the village but had crossed the river farther down at an island where Milremi had formerly lived, & that they were to go to Rama Kukam's by way of Magomero. From the slow rate at which they have begun their journey, it may be long enough ere they return with letters for us.

D.L. went ashore after breakfast & was received by Maponda rising from the midst of his counsellors & advancing to shake hands. Medicine was asked for a bad cough & large belly. When told to leave off drinking pombé, the mention of the word was enough to bring out at once the drunkard's opposition. He presented a large he-goat and wished Mr Y. to visit him. Mr Y. went ashore & presented him with a large coloured blanket & red umbrella. The blanket he threw round his shoulders, put up the u. & strutted off to shew himself to his wives. A small goat was then presented by Maponda. He shewed us cloth & supplies of which he wished sent to him from England. He wished medicine for his wives, that he might have more children. He has 90 wives. He was pressed to send the boys of his villages to the N. to be educated. Half consented. Started fr. M's & anchored in the entrance of the lake to be free of mosquitoes.

The varied countries of the Empire provided scope for the energies and talents of many individuals. Scottish experiences abroad were recorded in a number of ways: this is a page from the diary of Robert Laws of the Livingstonia Mission. This Church of Scotland mission, founded in memory of David Livingstone, was the first Scottish mission in what is now Malawi. Some of the difficulties of missionary life are related here – fever, problems with travel and communications, mosquitoes.

Diaries, letters, memoirs, drawings and, in the latter part of the 19th century, photography, all contribute to our understanding of the Scot abroad.

SCOTTISH PHOTOGRAPHERS ABROAD
DURING THE NINETEENTH CENTURY

A D Morrison-Low

It has been said that Scotland's most famous export is her people, and almost as soon as it was possible for them to take cameras abroad with them, amongst the travellers, diplomats, soldiers, merchants — all the people necessary to run an empire — there were a few practising the new art of photography. This was not easy in the earliest days, as the equipment and chemistry were both cumbersome and relatively expensive: before the coming of the railways only the idle rich could afford to travel for pleasure. Not until the 1880s was there a cheap, portable camera for the masses, and although travel books had excited curiosity since the eighteenth century, until after the First World War most people had little idea of what lay beyond their own locality. The Scottish photographer abroad seems to have come from various backgrounds; besides the wealthy amateur, who was part of a longer tradition of sight-seeing dilettantism, there was the Scottish emigrant who left home to set up professionally somewhere in the Empire, or other foreign parts. Not a few outstanding nineteenth century photographers turn out on closer inspection to have been of Scottish extraction. A third group consisted of the home-based professional who left Scotland briefly for a variety of reasons to make photographic excursions in foreign parts, returning to publish the results. And there were exceptions to all these rather artificial categories, who mixed elements of each, producing his own inimitable work.

A history of Scottish photography has yet to be written, and even when this has happened, it will be unlikely that all great Scottish photographers will be identified and their work appreciated: too much has been lost in the years between the invention of photography in 1839 and the setting up of a national Scottish archive in 1984 to study the results.

Photography was invented almost simultaneously in England and France, and made public in 1839. The French daguerreotype was a tricky, not to say unhealthy chemical process which produced a single, unique, reversed positive image of mercury-silver amalgam droplets suspended on a metal surface, so fragile that it had to be protected by a glass cover. In contrast, the English calotype consisted of a paper negative which, with due care, could be used frequently to produce as many positive paper prints as desired — the real drawback of the method felt by contemporaries was that the paper fibres gave a coarse-grained effect better used for landscapes while the daguerreotype reflected a mirror-like reality suitable for portraits.

However, no daguerreotypes taken by Scots abroad seem to have survived, although certainly some were taken. The method was anyway less popular with amateurs than the calotype process. During the 1840s a dissenting clergyman Dr Alexander Keith visited the Holy Land on a number of occasions to research material for a new edition of his book, *Evidence of the Truth of the Christian Religion*.

His eldest son, Dr George Skene Keith, an amateur photographer, took along his daguerreotype camera and the new edition used eighteen of these as the basis for engravings. The original daguerreotypes are lost.

The more popular calotype fared better and examples survive to show the excellent quality both in composition and technique from the earliest days. Although the most famous Scottish calotype partnership, the professionals D O Hill and Robert Adamson was between 1843 and 1848 firmly based in Edinburgh, some amateurs did go to the Continent, amongst them an Edinburgh lawyer, George Moir, one of the founder members of the Edinburgh Calotype Club, who took some early calotypes in Ghent. John Muir Wood (1805-92) came from a musical family: his father was a musical instrument-maker while he himself and his brother were music sellers and publishers based in Edinburgh. In his youth he had received musical tuition on the Continent, in Paris and Vienna, and besides becoming a competent linguist he had formed a wide circle of acquaintances. Throughout his life he was evidently much struck by beautiful scenery, and he took up calotyping to try to capture on paper what he saw on his travels, although he is not known to have attempted either sketching or painting. John Muir Wood seems to have taken up photography during the period 1843 to 1845, but it is not known whether he was self-taught or learnt from someone: he was certainly an experienced photographer by the time of his Belgian visit in 1847 from which many calotypes survive, some of the earliest taken in that country. The invention of the calotype co-incided with a period when he had no family responsibilities — he did not marry until 1851 — and was supported by an expanding concern, run primarily by his very competent brother. His diary for 1847 gives a brief account of his trip to Belgium with some details of his calotype activities, and the surviving prints give some indication of his ability. However, with increased business commitments and family ties he appears to have dropped photography as suddenly as he had taken it up.

Leith-born Fredrick William Flower (1815-89) emigrated to Oporto, Portugal at the age of nineteen, where he worked for a company shipping port, and then later ran and owned his own shipping business. For about ten years between 1850 and 1860 he used the calotype process to take photographs as a hobby in and around Oporto. Born in Kirkmichael, Ayrshire, John MacCosh (1805-85) was an army surgeon with the Bengal Division of the East India Company's Army; he photographed his last two campaigns, the 2nd Sikh War (1848-9) and the 2nd Burma War (1852-3), the earliest war photographer in Europe and Asia. His calotypes, which were taken when he was off-duty, show fellow officers and wives, portraits of the local population, and captured guns and buildings — of war conditions, rather than battle, a concept of war photography which came later in the Crimea.

Like John MacCosh, John Murray (1809-98) was another medical officer with the British East India Company who took photographs in India, starting about 1849. A farmer's son from Blackhouse, Aberdeen, Murray produced large-scale waxed paper negatives printed on both albumen and salted papers, mostly of views of Agra and its vicinity, and the northwestern provinces of India, which were published for him in London. Evidently there were others, camera in hand, or on the shoulders of a native servant, travelling around Asia at the time. In 1882 the Minute Book of the Edinburgh Photographic Society noted that a Dr Alexander Hunter showed a large number of calotypes taken in Burma thirty years before, mostly of architectural remains. On other occasions he discussed photographs taken in India, but as yet his photographic career remains obscure.

In 1851 a new photographic method was made public: the wet collodion process. This faster, sharper form of photography, unhindered by patents, meant the real beginning of a photographic industry, and soon photographs became cheap enough for all but the poorest. Although amateurs continued to travel about the world, taking scenic views as souvenirs, more professionals did the same to sell to both travellers and those who remained at home. Robert Macpherson (1811-72) had been born and educated in Edinburgh, but left for Rome for health reasons in the early 1840s. He took up photography in 1851 and became immensely successful, selling his views to British visitors at a time when Rome was popular as a winter resort. William Carrick (1827-78) had also been born in Edinburgh, but was taken to Russia at the age of a few months, where his family ran a timber merchant business near St Petersburg. Carrick returned to Scotland in 1857, where he persuaded John Macgregor, a photographic technician, to return with him to set up a studio Besides making a living through portraiture, Carrick also made a photographic record of his adopted country, his 'Russian Types', whom he managed to make look relaxed and natural.

Another Scotsman who pursued documentary photography was John Thomson (1837-1921), whose early life is obscure, although he seems to have studied at Edinburgh University. From 1862 to 1872 he travelled in the Far East, which resulted in the publication of *The Straits of Malacca, Indo-China and China* (London, 1875). His other travel books, among them *The Antiquities of Cambodia* (Edinburgh, 1867), *Illustrations of China and Its People* (London, 1873-4) and *Through Cyprus with a Camera* (London 1879) were to a certain extent overshadowed by the somewhat controversial and famous project, *Street Life in London,* a social documentary first issued in twelve monthly instalments in 1877-8.

Besides being able to use photography to illustrate books, the wet collodion process enabled other forms of cheap illustration which were to some extent fostered by the photographic industry — the carte-de-visite, the stereophotograph, and the picture postcard all saw their heydey during Victoria's reign. John James Reilly (1838-94) was born in Glasgow but emigrated to California in 1856; by 1863 he had become a photographer of 'Photographic Views' for the stereoscope at Niagara Falls. From there he moved to the Yosemite Valley, then to San Francisco and subsequently to Marysville, California, producing some thousands of views for the stereoscopic market. Back in Scotland, the postcard industry had grown out of the demand firstly for view prints, and then stereo pairs: the two main businesses being that of George Washington Wilson (1823-93) based in Aberdeen and James Valentine (1815-80) in Dundee. Wilson's firm eventually published views from all round the world, and one of his employees, Frederick Hardy, who emigrated to South Africa, found that with work unobtainable, he could send photographs of street scenes and diamond mining back to Aberdeen for publication by Wilson. Eventually he moved to Australia, where he continued to supply Wilson with portraits of aborigines. George

Russian peasants in
Simbirsk, 1871.
Albumen print by
William Carrick.
(National Galleries of
Scotland)

a Train in the snow [handwritten caption]

Train in the snow, Canada. Albumen print by Alexander Henderson, who became a professional photographer in the 1860s. (National Galleries of Scotland)

Dobson Valentine (1852-90) left for New Zealand for health reasons in the mid 1880s, which meant that the family firm lost one of its best photographers. In New Zealand Valentine continued to take photographs which were sold by an Auckland publisher in albums or as loose prints. Two years after his death, an unidentified Valentine 'representative' took some 450 inferior views which later found their way back to the Dundee headquarters, unlike those of George Dobson Valentine which have been lost.

For others, the act of emigration was a clean break. For instance, Alexander Gardner (1821-82) was born in Paisley but emigrated to the United States in 1856, where he learned photography, and joined Matthew Brady's organisation before setting up on his own. His most famous images are of the American Civil war which helped to bring home the brutality of battle and the effect of the war on American society: these were published in *Gardner's Photographic Sketchbook of the War* (Washington DC, 1886). Gardner went on to become official photographer for the Union Pacific Railroad in 1867, for whom he produced documentary pictures of railroad life. Joseph Collier (1836-1910) was originally a blacksmith from Loanhead, Aberdeenshire, who became interested in photography after an injury around 1856. Emigrating with his family in 1871, he had intended to go to Australia but a letter from a cousin advised him to go to a thriving gold-mining farm, Central City, Colorado. There he ran a successful photographic business, moving to Denver in 1878. He travelled all over the state, one of the first photographers to capture the world famous beauty of the Colorado mountains.

William Notman (1826-91) was for many years Canada's most famous photographer, and the first to have an international reputation. Born, like Gardner, in Paisley, he emigrated in 1856, settling in Montreal where he opened a photographic studio which was so successful that in time the business had branches all over Canada, and eight in the United States. He himself is famous chiefly for portraits, although documentary scenes from contemporary life also formed a large part of his work. On a less grand scale was the work of Alexander Henderson (1831-1913), a Scots-born accountant who emigrated to Canada in 1855, and who seems to have taken up photography about three years later. From the beginning landscape was his passion, and he turned professional in 1866 or 1867, opening a studio in Montreal. For several years he was Manager of the Canadian Pacific Railway Photography Department and was one of the few in Canada able to make a commercial success out of outdoor photography.

All over the world nineteenth century Scotsmen were taking photographs almost from the moment of invention: further research may well unearth a few Scotswomen behaving similarly. The quality of their work, unremarked until recently by their countrymen, has been amongst the highest produced and deserves further study and appreciation.

The attractions of the picturesque, to both photographers and tourists, grew in the 19th century, and the Highlands were increasingly visited. They were also an attraction to the geologist. Scotland was of immense interest to early geologists because of the variety of its rocks and the very long time spans they represent. These isolated relict hills of Torridonian Sandstone, seen from the northeast of Stoer, Sutherland, overlie some of the oldest known rocks in Britain. These, the rocks in the foreground, are over 2400 million years old. One of the foremost Scottish geologists in the 19th century was Hugh Miller.

HUGH MILLER

Charles D Waterston

Enterprise is the child of tension as surely as necessity is the mother of invention. Necessity and tension, however, are born of suffering. To the enterprising the perception of tensions, social or intellectual, acts as a goad from which relief can be found only in change. For them the suffering which accompanies need and tension is intolerable. As Willian Pitt affirmed 'Necessity is . . . the argument of tyrants; the creed of slaves'. No enterprising spirit can rest content in the presence of such suffering. In Hugh Miller's words

> Contentment is certainly no virtue when it has the effect of arresting either individuals or peoples in their course of development; and is perilously allied to great suffering, when the men who exemplify it are so thoroughly happy amid the medeocrities of the present, that they fail to make provision for the contingencies of the future.

More often in practical matters the enterprising succeed, but in the realm of ideas it is frequently they who suffer. Hugh Miller was one who could not rest content amid the needs and tensions of his generation and fought and suffered to change the *status quo*.

Miller lived at the centre of a web of tensions. He embodied the lowland Scot and the highlander. Like many Scots living in the first half of the nineteenth century, Janus-like, he looked back on the old order of nationhood, clan loyalties and paternalistic land-ownership and forward to the bitter-sweet fruits of the Enlightenment now ripening into changed attitudes and expectations and the social upheaval of the industrial revolution. While deprecating the working conditions of the common man he shrank from the implications of organised labour and universal suffrage. He thrilled to the insights of science but held firmly to his faith in God and in man made in His image. He saw the church as a lamp to lighten the path of the nation but fought furiously to free it from established interests. Even in his marriage there was tension arising from the social differences between his wife and himself. His immense popularity was probably due to the fact that so many of his Scottish readers were touched by similar tensions and they admired, as we still may do, the manly honesty with which he tackled them in his writings. The bullet which ended his life did not end his influence. The way in which we live today in Scotland is due, in more ways than we may suspect, to the work of Hugh Miller.

Miller was born in Cromarty on 22nd October 1802. His father was a shipmaster, one of a long line of seafaring lowlanders. His mother was of highland stock descended on the distaff side from Donald Ross or Roy, well known in his day as a Gaelic seer in Sutherland. As highland and lowland blood pulsed in the veins of the boy, so highlanders and lowlanders mingled in the streets of Cromarty down which he ran. Then Cromarty was a busy port doing business over the waters of the Moray Firth with other Scottish ports,

Hugh Miller. (National Galleries of Scotland)

with England and the Continent. It was originally a lowland settlement but, since the break-up of the clan system, it had attracted highlanders seeking employment as labourers, farm servants, weavers or operatives in the hemp factory. The chapel which had been built in 1783 for these Gaelic speakers by George Ross, the proprietor of the lands of Cromarty, now stands roofless beside the Hugh Miller column overlooking the town. In Miller's day, its congregation of landless highlanders must have contrasted strangely with the 'English' congregation meeting below in Cromarty's old parish church where worshipped 'all its men of property and influence, from its merchants and heritors, down to the humblest class that afterwards became its ten-pound franchise holders'.

When Hugh was only five, Captain Miller was lost with his ship. His mother had to take in needlework to support him and his two baby sisters. He went to school but disliked the dominie and was frequently excluded or played truant. Despite this he was at school for ten years and Dr Mackay Mackenzie has pointed out that he was promoted to the Latin class which was reserved for the brightest pupils. He had at his disposal some 450 volumes and he must have read extensively during these early years. What he may have missed in formal education was made good by his maternal uncles. James Wright fired his imagination by sharing his own interest in history and antiquities while Alexander, his much loved Uncle Sandy, encouraged him in his study of nature as together they explored the shores, cliffs, fields and woodlands of the Black Isle. His uncles were disappointed when, at the age of 17, Hugh decided to become apprenticed to a stonemason rather than go to college. His decision may have been influenced by his mother's circumstances, since three years earlier tragedy had again struck her family when her two little girls had died of fever. Only Hugh was left to Harriet and, in the years that he was apprenticed, she remarried.

Miller worked as a stonemason for 15 years, the first three of which he was apprenticed to his step-uncle. He travelled widely following his trade to the east and west coasts of Ross-shire. He spent some time during 1824-5 in Edinburgh, where he met the lowland labourer for the first time and became involved in a strike. Although he romanticised the stonemason's craft in his writings, it is clear from his account of it given to Principal Baird, five years before he gave it up, how hard the life was. With hands chapped and bleeding in the cold of winter, with the underlying misery of bothy life overglossed with an artificial gaiety, sometimes with nowhere to sleep except in a knocked-up shelter and with the rot of silicosis working in his lungs, it is little wonder that his health broke down and latterly he could do only light work. It was while carving a tombstone in 1831 that he met Lydia Fraser who became his wife six years later.

Miller had produced a small book of poems in 1829, but the prose pieces which he wrote for the *Inverness Courier* in the same year entitled 'Letters on the Herring Fishery' were much more successful and encouraged him to cultivate his talents of authorship. In 1834 his friend Robert Ross, who had just been appointed agent of the bank in Cromarty, invited him to become an accountant in the Commercial Bank. After their marriage Miller had intended to emigrate with Lydia to America, but this offer gave him a chance to develop as a writer and to establish himself in a position more fitting to the husband of a gentle wife and so the offer was accepted. That Hugh Miller had not already sailed on one of the emigrant ships which were then leaving Cromarty and other northern ports was probably because he wished to see his volume of 'Traditions' through the press. Since 1829 he had been recording the folk legends of the north and had collected them in a work which he claimed to have modelled on White's *Natural History of Selbourne*. When Miller had been in Edinburgh in 1824, Robert Chambers' *Traditions of Edinburgh* had been published and the following year T Crofton Croker's *Fairy Legends and Traditions of the South of Ireland* had appeared and these may well have encouraged him to form his own collection. *Scenes and Legends of the North of Scotland* was published in 1835 and was well reviewed.

Many would have found contentment at work behind the banker's desk and at home among a growing family. Not so Hugh Miller. He sought intellectual fulfilment among the rocks and fossils around Cromarty and, finding that a salary of £100 a year did not go as far as he once thought it would, his wife took in pupils while he supplemented the family income by writing articles. It was not long, however, before his fury at events which were overtaking the Church

of Scotland reached flash point and the explosion which followed
was heard throughout the land and shattered, once and for all, the
tranquillity of his family life.

A religious man, Miller had become interested in church politics
through his friend Alexander Stewart, parish minister of Cromarty.
The law of patronage had been re-established in Scotland during the
last Parliament of Queen Anne under which ministers were
appointed to livings in the Church of Scotland by the patrons and
were not, except under special circumstances, referred to the wishes
of the congregation. For Thomas Chalmers and the Evangelical Party
within the Church which he led, this transgressed religious conviction. Miller sympathised with the congregation of Auchterarder
whose wishes had been overruled on appeal in the House of Lords in
the latest patronage case at which Lord Brougham had supported the
status quo. He expressed his feelings in an article entitled 'Letter
from one of the Scottish People to the Right Honourable Lord
Brougham and Vaux, on the opinions expressed by his Lordship on
the Auchterarder Case' and sent it to Robert Paul, manager of the
Commercial Bank in Edinburgh, who was persuaded to have it
printed by Dr Robert Candlish. Little wonder that the article commanded the attention of the leaders of the Evangelical Party for, with
a popular authority, a confident faith and in striking language, it ably
set out the non-intrusion argument. This, together with 'The Whigg-
ism of the Old School', a pamphlet which Miller had published in the
same year (1839), revealed a force existing in Cromarty which could
be harnessed to drive the engine of the Evangelical Party. In the
following year Miller was asked to come to Edinburgh as editor of
the Party's new twice-weekly newspaper *The Witness* and, for the
remaining 16 years of his life, he became identified with that paper.
His standing with the Evangelical Party grew steadily and his articles,
breathing as they did the fire of conviction in the rightness of the
cause, won a wide readership. In the election of 1841 it had been
claimed that all but one of the Scottish parliamentary candidates
were advocating some popular modification of patronage. So effective was *The Witness* in rallying support that, when the Disruption of

the Church of Scotland took place in 1843, one third of the membership left the Established Church to found the Church of Scotland Free. Hugh Miller had well earned the prominence he was given in Hill's well-known picture of the first assembly of the Free Church at Tanfield Hall.

From the beginning Hugh Miller made *The Witness* his own. In his first year as editor he serialised his writings on the Old Red Sandstone and most of his geological works, which later appeared in book form, first appeared in the pages of that paper. Although brilliantly written, they can hardly have been what the fathers of the Free Kirk had expected from their Edinburgh newspaper. For Miller, however, the theological issues raised by the new science of geology were important and his wide readership showed that the public shared his interest. After the Disruption the independent stance adopted by Miller's editorials proved too much for an influential section of the Free Church. In 1847 Dr Candlish, who had done so much to bring Miller to Edinburgh, said that he could not open the paper 'without a feeling of dread lest something untoward should be in it' and complained that there was no 'taste or tact' shown in the handling of public questions. He and his friends believed that *The Witness* should become more exclusively a Church paper and more an exponent of Whig opinion than it was. It was even suggested that Free Church papers in other cities, such as the *Glasgow Guardian,* should be amalgamated with *The Witness* and that the editor should work under the direction of a central church committee. That editor should not be Hugh Miller. In 1845, however, *The Witness* had become the property of Miller and of his business partner Robert Fairly and they could not be easily dislodged. Miller fought back and, with the support of Dr Chalmers, the independence of the paper was upheld. Although *The Witness* became more and more isolated from the Free Church leadership, it remained popular with the people. Miller's heart-beat was its pulse, however, and the paper did not long survive his death.

Miller was a well-known and popular character in the capital. Sir Archibald Geikie described him at this time as

. . . broad shouldered, clad in a suit of rough tweed, with a shepherd's plaid across his chest and a stout stick in his hand. His shock of sandy-coloured hair escaping from under a soft felt hat, his blue eyes either fixed on the ground or gazing dreamily ahead, seemed to take no heed of their surroundings. His rugged features wore an expression of gravity, softening sometimes into a smile and often suffused with a look of wistful sadness, while the firmly compressed lips betokened strength and determination of character.

D O Hill's famous calotypes confirm that general impression. In her reflections on Miller, Marion Wood wrote of his eyes as pale and sad — 'the saddest I ever knew'. 'He was somewhat shy and proud and jealous of his independence and some found him inaccessible from this cause.' Perhaps these characteristics were bred of the Democratic Intellect and were shared by such men as his famous contemporary Thomas Carlyle.

Hugh Miller's writing is enlivened with humour, suffused with geniality and sometimes hot with righteous indignation at perceived evil. Sometimes, however, the sun is hidden by impenetrable clouds and darkness and his work assumes the terror of the apocalyptic, as in 'A Vision of the Railroad', or the fear of the occult. There was a weird streak in his personality which showed in morbidity, in his fevered hallucinations so minutely described, in his belief in ghosts and fairies, and in later life in a growing fear of personal attack. Robert Dick, the Thurso baker, geologist and botanist, to whom Miller owed so much, said of him 'Poor Hugh! . . . He was sorely afflicted with his head while he was here, and to such a degree that neither you nor I can form any idea of his sufferings.' This black suffering eclipsed him in the end. In a scribbled note to Lydia he said '. . . a fearful dream rises upon me, I cannot bear the terrible thought . . . My brain burns . . . farewell'. He shot himself through the heart on Christmas Eve 1856. The news shook Scotland and thousands lined the route through Edinburgh which led to his last resting place in the Grange Cemetery.

Have the life and writings of this man any significance for us today? I would suggest five fields in which I believe Hugh Miller made a significant contribution to our heritage.

Firstly, as noted by Dr Mackay Mackenzie, Hugh Miller deserves credit as a folklorist, since in *Scenes and Legends* and *My Schools and Schoolmasters* he has saved for us so much about the character of the people of the north of Scotland that otherwise would have been lost. Miller had met people whose family traditions extended back to the seventeenth century. He collected their tales knowing that they were disappearing.

> The Sybiline tomes of tradition are disappearing in this part of the country one by one, and I find, like Selkirk in his island, when the rich fruits of autumn were dropping around him, that if I myself do not preserve them, they must perish.

Through his work we may still hear such stories as The Polander, The one-eyed Stepmother, The Charm of the Egg, The Guardian Cock, Sandison's Spulzie and The Washing of the Mermaid, the mere titles of which arouse curiosity. Not only did Hugh Miller enjoy the tales and the tellers, he also realised the ethnological significance of legend.

> Man in a savage state is the same animal everywhere, and his constructive powers, whether employed in the formation of a legendary story, or a battleaxe, seem to expatiate almost every- where in the same rugged track of invention. For even the tradi- tions of this first stage may be identified, like its weapons of war, all over the world.

Dr Mackenzie tells us that, where it has been possible to check. Miller's version of the Scottish legends against parallels in Europe, they have been accurately recorded. Because of the growing appreciation of the value of folk-studies, *Scenes and Legends* may be more in harmony with modern taste than it was when first published.

The second contribution which Hugh Miller made was to geology. As he himself wrote

> Such is the state of progression in geological science, that the geologist who stands still for but a very little must be content to find himself left behind.

His discovery of fossil fishes and plants in the Old Red Sandstone rocks of Cromarty, however, is an achievement which will stand the test of time. He discovered the Cromarty fish beds in August 1830 and began work on them in complete isolation. Similar fishes from Caithness had come to the notice of the scientific world in 1826 and in the following winter the fossil fishes of Gamrie in Banffshire had been found. Miller knew nothing of these events until Anderson's *Guide to the Highlands* appeared in 1834. This brought him into contact with George Anderson, Conservator of the Museum of the Northern Institution in Inverness, who confirmed the similarity of his Cromarty fossils with those of Gamrie. Mention of the Cromarty fish fossils in *Scenes and Legends,* published in the following year, attracted the attention of geologists who later came to Cromarty to see Miller's specimens. In this way he met Dr John Fleming, who had published in 1827 a notice of the first Old Red Sandstone fish fossil from the Midland Valley, and Dr John G Malcolmson who was to work with a remarkable group of kindred spirits on the fossil fishes of Moray, and through them he was put in touch with the celebrated Swiss ichthyologist, Louis Agassiz, and with Sir Roderick Murchison.

Two fishes which occur in the Cromarty fish beds, *Coccosteus* and *Pterichthyodes,* look very unlike modern fishes in that they had box-like bodies made up of a number of plates. It is little wonder that their remains were confused by the early workers and, in a recent Royal Scottish Museum publication, Dr Andrews has shown how Dr Malcolmson played an important part in recognising that two distinct fishes were involved. Miller took an active part in this work and was able to distinguish the different bone patterns of both dorsal and ventral surfaces of *Pterichthyodes.* Thus, when *The Old Red Sandstone* was published in book form in 1841, the Cromarty fishes were described and illustrated in a meaningful way. This was a remarkable achievement by Miller, a self-educated palaeontologist, and accomplished in only six years from his first report of his discovery.

Other geological achievements were his discovery of some 50 species of plants in the Jurassic rocks of the Helmsdale/Golspie district, his discovery of the reptile bed on Eigg and his description of Robert Dick's fossils from Caithness in *Footprints of the Creator.* He also had an interest in the post-glacial brick clays of the Forth. During his years in Cromarty and Edinburgh, and in the course of his holiday journeys, he amassed a major geological collection which, after his death, was acquired for the nation by public subscription and government grant. It is one of the most important collections in the Geology Department of the Royal Museum of Scotland and supplies material for study by scholars throughout the world.

Miller was attracted to geology by the sense of wonder which the beauty of stones and fossils excited in him:

> ... in a nodular mass of bluish-grey limestone ... I laid open my first-found ammonite. It was a beautiful specimen, graceful in its curves as those of the Ionic volute, and greatly more delicate in its sculpturing; and its bright cream-coloured tint, dimly burnished by the prismatic hues of the original pearl, contrasted exquisitely with the dark grey of the matrix which enclosed it ... I can scarce hope to communicate to the reader, after the lapse of so many years, an adequate idea of the feeling of wonder which the marvels of this deposit excited in my mind, wholly new as they were to me at the time.

That sense of wonder never left him and he was able to share it with his readers through his vivid descriptions, striking similes and simple language. It is doubtful whether any popular science writer has enjoyed such success. C C Gillispie claimed that by the end of the nineteenth century *The Testimony of the Rocks* had sold 42,000 copies, *Footprints of the Creator* had been through 17 editions and geology as one of the most popular sciences of the nineteenth century and one which could be enjoyed by all classes of society.

Hugh Miller's geology was part of his search for truth and it is characteristic of his writing that geology and theology should be argued together. I would place Miller's exploration of the interface of science and religion as his third contribution which deserves our interest and respect.

James Hutton, 'the father of modern geology', died in Edinburgh only five years before Miller's birth. He had been a central figure in the Scottish Enlightenment and his famous *Theory of the Earth* had been seen as a refurbishment, in geological colours, of the concept of the cosmos as a law-abiding machine which was the product of such pioneer scientists as Copernicus, Galileo and Newton. Already the rationality of nature had been applied by some to human activities and the perfection of man and society could be seen more in the power of reason than in divine providence. Indeed to some, but not to Hutton, God had become a debatable hypothesis. Others, believing that the orderliness of nature showed that it must have been conceived by a rational mind, affirmed that the mind of the creator God could be discovered in the character of the created order. This was the basis of Natural Theology and William Paley's famous statement of that belief was published in the year of Miller's birth.

The growth of rationalism led to reaction. The Romantic Movement in art and literature championed the value of imagination and intuition, over against reason, in the search for truth. Blake, Turner and Scott were all Miller's senior contemporaries. In religion this was paralleled by an emphasis on the value of personal spiritual experience and the Evangelical Party, to which Miller belonged, was strongly influenced by this renewed sense of pietism.

It is easy to understand the tensions which these conflicting movements would arouse in Miller as an honest man convinced of the value of the rationality of science and yet aflame with experiential religion. Not for him the anti-intellectual retreat into fundamentalism which has re-established itself as a perverse feature of our own day in many faiths. He warned that the truths of scripture should not be pledged on such things as the Mosaic account of creation or the Noachian deluge which science has disproved. He warned also that 'No true geologist ever professes to deduce his geology from Scripture'. He thought hard about the nature of truth as it may be discovered both in science and through religious insight and was concerned to answer 'the various questions which the old theology of Scotland has been asking for the last few years of the newest of the sciences'.

As stratigraphical palaeontology developed it became clear that the fauna and flora of the earth had changed through time. Many geologists followed the French palaeontologist, Cuvier, in supposing that periodic catastrophies had wiped out all or many then living things which had been replaced by newly created forms. Man could thus be seen as the highest species to appear in the latest of these successive creations. In 1830, however, Sir Charles Lyell brought to the notice of English-speaking readers the developmental hypothesis of Lamarck which postulated the inheritance of acquired characters and challenged the concept of the fixity of species. Miller first argued against this idea in the third chapter of *The Old Red Sandstone*. In 1844 the first edition of Robert Chambers' remarkable book, *Vestiges of Creation,* appeared anonymously. It traced an evolutionary principle throughout inorganic and organic nature. He wrote:

> The simplest and most primitive type under a law to which that of like-production is subordinate, gave birth to the type next above it, that this again produced the next higher order, and so on to the very highest, the stages of advance being in all cases very small — namely for one species only to another.

Hugh Miller wrote *Footprints of the Creator* as a counterblast to *Vestiges of Creation.* In it he developed the argument he had used in *The Old Red Sandstone* that, while fossils in each geological epoch do show advance from those going before, nevertheless he believed (erroneously) that within each epoch no such advance could be seen, indeed it was possible 'to get up as unexceptionable a theory of degradation as of development'. Miller's argument was flawed scientifically because of his misunderstanding of Old Red Sandstone stratigraphy. While geological evidence satisfied him as to the error of the *Vestiges,* his objections arising from its challenge to the dignity of man, however, were characteristic and written from the heart.

> If, during a period so vast as to be scarce expressible by figures, the creatures now human have been rising by almost infinitesimals, from compound microscopic cells . . . until they have at length become men and women whom we see around us, we must hold either the monstrous belief that all vitalities, whether those of nomads or of mites, of fishes or of reptiles, of birds or of beasts, are individually inherently immortal and undying, or that human souls are *not* so. The difference between . . . the spirit of the brute . . . and the spirit of man . . . is not a difference infinitesimally, or even automatically *small.* It possesses all the breadth of eternity to come, and it is an *infinitely great* distance.

In the *Testimony of the Rocks,* Miller carried his ideas further in suggesting that successive geological epochs could be interpreted as 'prophetic days' of long duration reflecting the biblical 'days' of creation. The present 'day' was to be likened to the seventh or Sabbath when man must be redeemed preparatory to the last day of everlasting life. As Dr Rudwick has observed, Miller's vision of the span of geological history as an eschatalogical future Kingdom of Christ marked him off from his geological contemporaries. In Gillispie's words, 'This may not be science strictly speaking — or even loosely speaking — but it is Christianity.' It was three years after Miller's death that Darwin published *The Origin of Species.* If Miller did not manage to provide the answers, his work was prophetic in identifying the questions which are raised by the issues of science and religion and which are still debated.

Miller's fourth major contribution to our heritage was the part he played in church politics. In these days of ecumenicism can we really claim that the Disruption of the Church of Scotland was a good thing? As we know things did not work out for church life in Scotland as the leaders of the Evangelical Party had hoped and, as the years went by, sectarianism became worse confounded. There is no doubt, however, that the Free Church of Scotland breathed a new spirit and missionary zeal into church life in this land and, because of what happened at the Disruption and as history has unfolded, the re-united Church of Scotland today enjoys a degree of self-determination *vis-a-vis* the State which is the envy of many a national church. Indeed it may be claimed that the inhibitions still imposed by the State upon the Church of England themselves constitute a stumbling block to ecumenical advance. Lastly we note Miller's contribution as an independent journalist. The large number of articles which he wrote covers the whole range of public interest of his day — historical and biographical, political and social, literary and scientific. To a modern reader it is striking how many of the political questions which he took up still concern us. The peace movement, the deserving and the idle poor, the nature of religious education in schools, the need for improved housing conditions for working people in town and country. The aggressor in Afghanistan in Miller's day, as he saw it, was Britain and he was not afraid to say so. Other topics such as the tragedy of the clearances in Sutherland and Rhum, which he described so graphically, the evils of the Bothie System and the repressive nature of the Game Laws were causes of his own day.

Our view of political questions is so conditioned by hackneyed party dogma and accepted wisdom that Hugh Miller's leading articles on the same questions speak with a surprising freshness and originality to the modern reader. Here is a cry for reform but not the voice of socialist materialism. Here is a cry for the retention of trusted values and institutions but not the voice of conservative self-interest. Here rather is an expression of an independent spirit of the Free Church of Scotland and the opinions are not always predictable, indeed they are sometimes apparently contradictory, but they are interesting and stimulating. As we have seen, it was the challenge to the dignity of man as a spiritual being, distinct from the brute creation, that so angered Miller in the development theory of organic evolution. It was the affront to the dignity of man as a spiritual being that always angered Miller whether that affront came from poor housing conditions and repressive government or landlords on the one hand, or from supine pauperism and overriding workers' power leading to strikes on the other. It is this regard for the worth of the spiritual man, be he aristocrat or artisan, which had for long been a glory of the Scottish People and which was rekindled in the Free Church of Scotland but which today is in eclipse. It is this that blazes out in Miller's best political journalism, as in his condemnation of the Bothie System:

> We have seen more than the mere outside of bothies, and know > from experience, that though they may be fit dwellings for hogs > and horses, they are not fit dwellings for immortal creatures, who > begin in this world their education for eternity.

INDEX

FURTHER READING

The following is a selected list of books which for the most part are readily available.

Brander, Michael *The Emigrant Scots* 1982

Bumsted, J M *The Scots in Canada* 1982

Cage, R A (ed.) *The Scots Abroad* Labour, Capital, Enterprise 1750-1914 1985

Calder, Angus *Revolutionary Empire*. The Rise of the English-speaking Empires from the Fifteenth Century to the 1780s 1981

Campbell, R H *Scotland Since 1707*. The Rise of an Industrial Society 1971

Clement, A G and R H S Robertson *Scotland's Scientific Heritage* 1961

Daiches, D (ed.) *A Companion to Scottish Culture* 1981

Davis, G E *The Democratic Intellect*. Scotland and Her Universities in the Nineteenth Century 1961

Devine, T M *The Tobacco Lords*. A Study of the Tobacco Merchants of Glasgow and Their Trading Activities 1975

Dickson, W K *The Life of Major-General Sir Robert Murdoch Smith* 1901

Donaldson, Gordon
The Scots Overseas 1966
Scotland: The Shaping of a Nation 1974

Ferguson, William *Scotland 1689 to the Present Day* 1968

Fletcher, Harold R and William H Brown *The Royal Botanic Garden Edinburgh 1670-1970* 1970

Gibb, Andrew Dewar *Scottish Empire* 1937

Hook, Andrew *Scotland and America*. A Study of Cultural Relations 1750-1835 1975

Hume, J P and M Moss *Clyde Shipbuilding from Old Photographs* 1975

Johnson, Robert E *Sir John Richardson* 1976

Kerr, A W *History of Banking in Scotland* 1926

Laffin, John *Scotland the Brave: The Story of the Scottish Soldier* 1963

Lenman, Bruce *An Economic History of Modern Scotland* 1977

Livingston, David *Missionary Travels and Researches in South Africa* 1857

Macmillan, D S *Scotland and Australia 1788-1850*. Emigration, Commerce and Investment 1967

Mair, Craig *A Star for Seamen* 1978

Munro, R W *Scottish Lighthouses* 1979

Mitchison, Rosalind *A History of Scotland* 1970

Newman, Peter C *Company of Adventurers* 1985

Nicholson, Christopher *Rock Lighthouses of Britain* 1983

Notestein, W *The Scot in History* 1946

Orel, Harold, Henry L Snyder and Marilyn Stokstad *The Scottish World*. History and Culture of Scotland 1981

Pearce, G L *The Scots of New Zealand* 1976

Phillipson, N T and Rosalind Mitchison (eds.) *Scotland in the Age of Improvement* 1970

Reid, W Stanford (ed.) *The Scottish Tradition in Canada* 1976

Rich, E E *History of the Hudson's Bay Company* 195

Ross, M J *Ross in the Antarctic* 1982

Sheilds, John *Clydebuilt: A History of Shipbuilding on the Clyde* 1949

Slaven, Anthony and S G Checkland (eds.) *Dictionary of Scottish Business Biography* 1986

Smailes, Helen *Scottish Empire*. Scots in Pursuit of Hope and Glory 1981

Smith, Robert Murdoch *Persian Art*. South Kensington Museum Art Handbook 1876

Guide to the Persian Collection. Edinburgh Museum of Science and Art 1896

Smout, T C *A History of the Scottish People 1560-1830* 1969

Scottish Trade on the Eve of the Union 1963

Symon, J A *Scottish Farming, Past and Present* 1959

Thomson, George Malcolm *The North-West Passage* 1975